I WILL NOT PERISH

Understanding God and the Holy Trinity

DR. PHYLLIS GLASS

FOREWORD BY:

Bishop Henry Hearns
Pastor Emeritus of Living Stone Cathedral of Worship
Mayor Emeritus of Lancaster, California, City Council

KNOWLEDGE POWER BOOKS

ISBN: 978-1-950936-37-3 (Paperback)
ISBN: 978-1-950936-38-0 (Ebook)
Library of Congress Control Number: Pending

Editor: Stacie Fujii
Cover Design: Angie Ayala
Interior Design: Jennifer Houle
Literary Director: Sandra L. Slayton

Published by:

KP Publishing
Valencia, CA 91355
www.kp-pub.com

Printed in the United States of America

FOREWORD

I have known Dr. Phyllis Glass for more than twenty-five years. She became a member of the First Missionary Baptist Church, where I served as the senior Pastor. I pastored for more than fifty-one years and within that time, Dr. Glass stood out due to her hunger and thirst for God's truth.

Dr. Glass was one of my stellar teachers, a minister who was always ready and prepared to present the Word of truth to one or many.

Dr. Glass has spent many hours planning and laying out the meaning and significance of the Godhead: Father, Son, and the third person, the Holy Spirit. In her writings, she has provided definitions for terms used so that the reader will have a comprehensive understanding of the power of the Godhead in the believer's life.

Dr. Phyllis Glass is a woman of good character and a friend of mine.

Bishop Henry Hearns
Pastor Emeritus of Living Stone Cathedral of Worship/FMBC
Mayor Emeritus of Lancaster, California, City Council

CONTENTS

PREFACE

There are several writings on the subject of the three parts of God, God the Father, Jesus Christ the Son, and the Holy Spirit, referred to as the Holy Trinity, that gives various views or opinions. Some have used the word *triune*, which is an ecclesiastical term that usually relates to the Christian church or its clergy and equates to the three parts of God. Since that term does not appear in any pages of the Bible or scriptures, I felt compelled to start a project that would give a life lesson, and increase the knowledge of any reader on one of the most profound yet intricate subject matters—The Holy Trinity: God the Father, God the Son, and God the Holy Spirit. I confess that embarking on this topic has been and can be a very difficult topic to explain, however I will provide a fairly easy but comprehensive explanation of the three tenets of the Trinity.

Included is a compilation of scripture to make understanding the concept of the complexities of the Holy Trinity easier.

My focus, as a retired teacher, is to encourage, provide meaningful content, and challenge those who may have a thirst for knowledge of the deeper things of God. My teaching experience has taught me that many types of writings on various subjects, or even the same subject can often offer a different biblical perspective all while providing a combination of truths and sources that is easily accessible. This book is written almost entirely using scriptural based references and provides an opportunity for the reader to research for their own personal validations of the interpretations contained herein.

As an apologist, meaning *one who defends the Word of God,* and because of my deep faith and belief in the Holy Scriptures, my prayers are for the reader to be even more enlightened and understand how the Trinity can impact their daily existence. Over the years, I have taught in church as well as junior and business college. The majority of this book is comprised of an exegesis of scripture, which gives *a critical explanation or interpretation of those Scriptures,* and are taken directly from the King James Version of the Bible. An exegesis will make clear the definition, purpose, and benefits of knowing and appreciating the Almighty God we love and serve.

The Bible, also called the "Living Word," is used to describe each person of the Trinity known as the Father, Son, and Holy Spirit. You will find the contents of the Bible will actually come alive as you discover all the attributes of each person.

This book is a result of two previous conversations, one, with a Christian associate, more than twenty years ago and held an important office in their church. He mentioned that he wasn't sure about "this trilogy thing." It was difficult for me to understand why someone at that level would question such a basic principle of the Christian faith.

The other conversation, more recently, with one of my grandsons. When I asked him what his interpretation of the Trinity was, he stated he was not as well versed as he would like to be.

After years of making both written and mental notes, I've concluded that there are many Christians in various phases of their lives, who do not have a clear understanding of the importance of the Godhead or Holy Trinity. But I do feel those encounters provided me with the opportunity to minister Genesis. 1:1 and John 1:1 addresses to the Holy Trinity. This book provides a condensed study guide material on how the three persons of the Holy Trinity work together. We should not take for granted the amount of understanding a Christian has or does not have about the things of God.

It is purposeful that all of the names or offices of the Trinity are not referenced in this book. I want to cause you, the reader to adhere to 2Timothy 2:15 which says,

> *"Study to show thyself approved unto God; a workman that needeth not to be ashamed, rightly dividing the word of truth."*

That is to seek out on your own in a quest to find those truths that coincide with the infallible Word of God. My intent is to maintain your concentration and interest in the subject matter. Only a select number of scriptures are being referenced which will in turn cause you to research on your own all of the characteristics that will express what each mean to you and how they have impacted your personal experiences. There are many benefits and rewards that come with the revelation knowledge one is able to uncover on their own.

INTRODUCTION

To understand the offices and functions of the Holy Trinity, one must first concede that God's plan from the beginning was drafted by all three persons of the Godhead or Holy Trinity.

It should be established that as Christians or believers in God, and in the Word of God, the Bible is where we obtain our truths. These truths are established repeatedly throughout the Bible without contradiction.

The term *Holy Trinity* is used to define the Godhead as being one God in three persons. The word "trinity" derives from the Latin word "trinitas" or "triad" meaning threefold. God the Father, in Christianity, is most referred to as God and is considered as the **first person** of the Trinity. The **second perso**n is God the Son (Jesus Christ), followed by the **third person** the Holy Spirit.

As Christians, we can have an assurance of the "eternal life" God promises. That assurance may come with many questions and/or concerns for Christians (believers) and non-believers. Those questions may include: what must I do to ensure that I will not perish? Do I need to reconsider my relationship with God? All Christians should know that receiving salvation is not the end of the road. It's just the beginning. We will address the truths revealed according to scriptures in the Bible to substantiate evidence of the Trinity.

The focus will center on how having in-depth knowledge of all three persons of the Trinity relate to understanding the heart of God. And how the significance of that revelation will forever impact your relationship with God.

You should know that knowledge of the Trinity has a direct bearing on one's salvation. God intends to make himself known, and how His plan was always to save us. That plan was also intended for us to know God as a divine being that includes the Father, the Son and the Spirit.

Revelation of the Trinity does not come automatically but requires a supernatural experience by those seeking knowledge through salvation. God did not make a formal declaration concerning the Trinity in words, but through deeds, His plan was not to leave us ignorant of His intentions. Knowledge of both the Old Testament and New Testament must be present to fully understand the Trinity.

The information inside these pages will show how we can hold to the promise that "whosoever believes" in Jesus Christ will not perish but have eternal life (John 3:16).

CHAPTER 1

TRUTHS REVEALED IN THE BIBLE

WHAT DOES BIBLE SCRIPTURE SAY ABOUT THE HOLY TRINITY?

The Bible addresses several times and provides proofs of there being a "Divine Trinity" or three separate and distinct persons in the Godhead. The Trinity is one of the main tenets of the Christian belief that one God is comprised of three persons: God the Father, God the Son, Jesus (who became flesh), and God the Holy Spirit. We accept that doctrine, by faith, they are all God, with the same divine characteristics. These truths, whether direct or indirect, are not contradictory and cannot be disregarded by anyone who has accepted the revelation that God gives through the Scriptures. The following are scriptures from both the Old and New Testaments that represent evidence and proofs of the Holy Trinity:

> **Isaiah 48:16** - *Come ye near unto me, hear ye this; I have not spoken in secret from the beginning; from the time that it was, there am I; and now the* ***Lord God****, and his* ***Spirit, hath sent me****.*

Isaiah 48:17 - *Thus saith the* ***Lord, thy Redeemer, the Holy One of Israel;*** *I am the Lord thy God which teacheth thee to profit, which leadeth thee by the way that thou shouldest go.*

In verses 16-17, the prophet Isaiah speaking under the anointing of God makes a clear and distinct reference to the Divine Trinity: the Lord God (one person), the Holy Spirit (another person) and the Messiah (still another person) that was sent by the two, being God and the Holy Spirit. Isaiah declares that from the time he was first called as a prophet, his mission was to publicly teach, preach, and speak the gospel.

1Peter 1:1 - *Peter an apostle of Jesus Christ, to the strangers scattered throughout Pontus, Galatia, Cappadocia, Asia, and Bithynia.*

1 Peter 1:2 - *Elect according to the foreknowledge of God the Father, through sanctification of the Spirit, unto obedience and sprinkling of the blood of Jesus Christ: Grace unto you, and peace, be multiplied.*

In verses 1-2, Peter's reference to "elect" is meant to single out a specific group considered to be God's "chosen". All men are called to become God's elect or chosen ones and can be if they will choose God. We are called to the obedience to Jesus, and to fulfill our purpose in three ways:

1. Through sanctification of the Spirit
2. Through our obedience to the gospel
3. Through sprinkling of the blood of Jesus Christ

Here Christians are encouraged by Peter as he communicates how special they are, and how much God loves them. He gives precise reference to the Trinity, and shows how each person of the Trinity is concerned with their salvation:

1. God the Father elects them
2. God the Son dies for them and sprinkles His blood on them
3. The Holy Spirit sanctifies them to make them holy.

One of the most significant references to the Trinity can be found in the first chapter of Genesis, which is the first book of the Bible. God establishes there is more than one participant in the making of man. The first sentence of Genesis 1:26 says:

And God said, Let us make man in our image, after our likeness:

Verse 27 - *So God created man in his own image, in the image of God created he him; male and female created he them.*

In verse 26, it's clear that these words were directed to someone. Those words were spoken by God the Father as he communicated with the Son and Holy Spirit. In sermon notes on this scripture, Chuck Smith[1] of the Blue Letter Bible Institute gives an excellent synopsis of this scripture which is in part as follows:

I. "SO GOD CREATED MAN IN HIS OWN IMAGE
   A. Note first of all that man was created. He did not evolve
      1. The evolutionist would have you to believe that man evolved over a period of billions of years by the fortunate occurrences of accidental circumstances.
      2. If we are indeed the product of blind random chance, billions of fortunate accidental circumstances, then there

---

1 Chuck Smith, BLB

is no real purpose of your existence is there? You came into this life by accident and chances are you will depart from this life by accident.

B. If on the other hand, we were created in the image and likeness of God, then there has to be a divine purpose for our existence.
    1. The Bible teaches that you are not the product of blind chance, but that you were designed by God who indeed has a divine purpose for your life.
    2. The Apostle Paul wrote to the church in Colosse:

Colossians 1:12 - *We give thanks unto the Father, who has made us fit to be partakers of the inheritance of the saints in light:*

Colossians 1:13 - *He has delivered us from the power of darkness, and has translated us into the kingdom of his dear Son:*

Colossians 1:14 - *In whom we have redemption through his blood, even the forgiveness of sins:*

Colossians 1:15 - *Who is the image of the invisible God, the firstborn over all creation:*

Colossians 1:16 - *For by him were all things created, that are in heaven, and that are in earth, visible and invisible, whether they be thrones, or dominions, or principalities, or powers; all things were created by him, and for him:*

Colossians 1:17 - *And he is before all things, and by him all things consist.*

3. Paul declared that we were created for Him.
4. In Revelation 4:11 it is declared that we were created for His good pleasure.

II. WHAT DOES IT MEAN IN THE IMAGE AND LIKENESS OF GOD?

A. First of all, the Bible tells us that God is a Spirit, and they that worship Him must worship Him in Spirit and in truth.

1. God is a superior trinity, Father Son and Holy Spirit
2. Man was created an inferior trinity, spirit, soul, and body.
3. It is in the realm of the Spirit that man meets and can commune with God.
    a. The Apostle Paul said that His Spirit bears witness with our spirit and that we are the sons of God.
    b. It is interesting that when Jesus who is the Son of God became man, as described for us in Philippians 2 Paul wrote.

Philippians 2:5 - *Let this mind be in you, which was also in Christ Jesus*

Philippians 2:6 - *Who, being in the form of God, thought it not robbery to be equal with God:*

Philippians 2:7 - *But made himself of no reputation, and took upon Him the form of a servant, and was made in the likeness of men:*

Philippians 2:8 - *And being found in fashion as a man, he humbled himself, and became obedient unto death, even the death of the cross.*

a. Note the He was in the form of God, whatever that form might have been, and was made in likeness of man.
b. John tells us that no man has seen God at any time, but the only begotten Son has manifested Him.
c. Jesus later said, "If you have seen Me, you have seen the Father."

B. We are created in the image of God in the spiritual sense.
1. God's chief emotional attribute is love, so God created us with a capacity to love.
2. God has the capacity to reason, so He created us with the ability reason.
3. God's chief governing characteristics is self-determination, so he created us with the capacity of self-determination.
4. God thinks, feels, wills, speaks, so He has created us with the capacity to think, feel, will and speak.

C. Here's what we can learn from our discernment and observation of the abilities and capacities that God has given us?
1. We have the capacity to understand the existence of God, therefore God evidently wanted us to know that He existed.
2. We can understand the concept of infinity. Thus, God must have wanted us to understand that He is infinite.
3. He created us with the capacity to fellowship with God, so He must have desired that we have fellowship with Him.

1 John 1:1 - *That One who was from the beginning, who we have heard, who we have seen with our eyes, who we have looked upon, and our hands have handled, of the Word of life;*

1 John 1:2 - *For the life was manifested, and we have seen, and bear witness, and shew unto you that eternal life, which was with the Father, and was manifested unto us*

1 John 1:3 - *That which we have seen and heard declare we unto, that ye also may have fellowship with us: and truly our fellowship is with the Father, and with his Son Jesus Christ.*

D. What was God's purpose in creating us? As we mentioned earlier for His good pleasure, but what is His good pleasure?
   1. First that we believe in Him. "For without faith, it is impossible to please God, for he that comes to God must first believe that He is and believe that He will reward those who diligently seek Him.
   2. God desired meaningful fellowship with His creation.
   3. God built into us the need to worship, so that we would worship Him.
   4. In the book of Romans, Paul tells us that God created us subject to emptiness, and that by design:
      a. Man has a built-in vacuum, and because nature cannot stand a vacuum, it always seeks to fill it.
      b. So, man is always seeking to fill the vacuum within.
      c. Only the One that designed that vacuum could fill it.
      d. Man tries to fill it with so many things. Sex, alcohol or drugs, things. Solomon tried everything, he said "that he did not withhold from himself one thing that his heart desired, yet he ended up with the cry of emptiness. Vanity, vanity, all is vanity and vexation of spirit."

5. Maybe you have been trying to fill the void in your life, and are hoping this newest adventure, or possession will do the trick. Jesus said to the woman who was trying to fill the void in her life with different men, "Drink of this water but you will thirst again, but if you drink of the water that I can give, you will never thirst again."
6. With this in mind, those who live their lives as a true believer in Christ are more inclined to not be striving or nor bickering, but living a Godly life satisfied, content, and at peace."

Because there are many scriptures that are mentioned, I have compiled a list of additional Bible verses that reference all three members of the Trinity in the back of this book.

WAS THE BIBLE INSPIRED?

The truths or scriptures of the Bible were inspired by God in various ways. While some scriptures are the words of God as He spoke them, other scriptures were recorded as the writer put those inspired words to pen as they received guidance from the Holy Spirit.

Several articles have been written expounding on the nature and role of the "Trinity" and is documented all throughout scripture. Although these articles are from different Christian denominations, they represent viewpoints that are consistent with the biblical definition of the Trinity. One such article written by Charles Stanley seems to provide one of the simpler ways to understand how the Trinity operates. Charles Stanley is the senior pastor of the First Baptist Church in Atlanta, Georgia. He is also the founder and president of In Touch

Ministries. The following excerpt was taken from *The Truth About the Trinity*[2] by In Touch Ministries as follows:

"The word Trinity cannot be found in the Bible but the truth of it can. While there's only one God, the Trinity consists of three distinct persons, the Father, Son, and Holy Spirit. All are equally omniscient, omnipotent, omnipresent, eternal, and unchanging, but each one has unique functions.

Scripture shows how each member of the Trinity fulfills a specific role and reveals how those three roles interrelate. Let me express this idea in these three terms:

1. The Father creates a plan,
2. Jesus Christ implements the plan, and
3. The Holy Spirit administers the plan.

All three members of the Trinity are fully God."

An article on the Trinity written by Dr David Jeremiah references 2Corinthians13:14 when he says, "This verse gives a beautiful picture of the Trinity: God who is one, existing eternally in three Persons – God the Father, God the Son, and God the Holy Spirit – interacting in a oneness that is dynamic and loving. Just as a human family works together in love to accomplish their goals, so God – three in one – acts to bring His people to Him and help them walk in righteousness. God the Father supplies love; God, the Son, Jesus Christ, supplies grace; God, the Holy Spirit, supplies communion and strength."[3] Dr David Jeremiah is the founder of Turning Point Radio and Television Ministries and senior pastor of Shadow Mountain Community Church in San Diego, California.

---

2 Charles Stanley
3 David Jeremiah

Joe Paprocki is National Consultant for Faith Formation at Loyal Press and has been involved in the catechetical ministry for over 35 years. An article from Joe's publication, *Cathechist Journey*, on "Explaining the Trinity"[4] by Lisa Jones in which she gives the following analogy:

"In the name of the Father and of the Son, and of the Holy Spirit" - these are words we use every time we pray the Sign of the Cross. Even young children know them. The prayer expresses the mystery of the Most Holy Trinity, that God reveals himself in Three Persons: the Father, Son and Holy Spirit.

The concepts of the Trinity can be difficult for anyone to understand, especially young children. St. Patrick famously explained the Trinity by relating God in Three Persons to the shamrock. A three-leaf clover has three lobes that are unique from each other but all part of the same clover or shamrock. They are three leaves, but on only one leaf.

Their questions reveal the difficulty in teaching and understanding the concept of the Holy Trinity. The children were trying so hard to understand how God can be "three persons" at one time. Yes, there is one God, and this God is our Father. This God is also the Father's Son, and God the Holy Spirit is the love that flows between the Father and the Son. This can be a little difficult to explain in a way that satisfies the curiosity of a third-grade class.

At some point, I simple had to tell the kids that it is OK if we do not fully understand the Trinity. That's what makes it a mystery: it can only be known through God's revelation. Sure, we can learn about the Trinity through his work in creation and in Scripture, but ultimately, it is something that we cannot understand through human reason alone. It can only be revealed by God through faith.

There are some things that we know are true because of our faith, even if we do not completely understand them. Our faith helps us believe and accept God's revelation, even when we do not fully understand these things with our

4 Lisa Jones, Joe Paprocki, Catechist Journey

rational minds. That is what we mean by the word mystery: it is something that can only be known through God's revelation. The mystery of the Most Holy Trinity is the source of all the mysteries of our faith."

There is proof that at least 40 or more writers of different backgrounds documented various books of the Bible over a timeframe of over hundreds of years. According to 2 Timothy 3:16-17: All scripture is given by inspiration of God, and is profitable for doctrine, for reproof, for correction, for instruction in righteousness: That the man of God may be perfect, thoroughly furnished unto all good works. So, while they used their own writing styles and expressions, those whose writing contributed to the Bible, recorded what God inspired them to record.

David Peach posted an article on Books of The Bible: "Complete List With Authors."[5] That article gives a list of the Books of the Bible in the Old Testament and New Testament arranged in groups based on the type of book. David Peach states, "In some cases the author is not absolutely known. I will first list the name of the commonly accepted author. If there are multiple people who possibly authored the book, I will list them in descending order of common acceptance. There is much debate on some of the authors and probably won't be definitively answered by us here."

The books are organized in a manner that gives understanding to the purpose and content and the complete list of all 66 books are listed in the back of this book.

It's important to stress these truths were divinely inspired because of how precisely all the books of the Bible coincide with one another. These books were compiled over a period of time without any coordination and/or collaboration from the writers. And yet, they all tell the same story, with the same conclusion and same consistency. No other book or writing in history have ever been able

5 David Peach

to rival the profound truths and revelations as the Bible. The inspired scriptures were purposely written so that the people of God would not perish.

PRINCIPLES OF INTERPRETING TRUTHS IN THE BIBLE

Before sense can be made on this topic, one should be open to accepting the Bible that represent the Word of God in a series of 66 books of what is considered to be God inspired. These 66 books represent the impact God had on the lives of men who received divine instruction in writing specific truths according to the Will of God.

Acceptance of the Bible as truth greatly depends on the belief that certain principles that cannot be disputed have been applied. Modern day interpretations on some subject matters would be based upon whatever the writer or reader decided it should be. For example, the truth lies in the eye of the beholder. That arbitrary manner of interpretation is not valid when using specific biblical theory to research truth for its intended meaning. The standards used to determine the accuracy of interpretation must be derived at carefully. Revelation of the infallible truths of scripture are significant to the Christian believer. For Biblical research, two of those principles and how they are applied are hermeneutics and exegesis.

The definition of exegesis, according to *The Lexicon Webster Dictionary*[6], Volume 1, *page 343*, is defined as being the "critical explanation or interpretation of Scripture."

The definition of hermeneutics, page 451 is "the art or science of interpretation, more specifically applied to Scriptures."

Bible scholar Godwin Goziem Jireh and Ingrid Harris, PhD[7] provide an excellent description of the differences between exegesis and hermeneutics. Their definitions are as follows:

6 The Lexicon Webster Dictionary

7 Godwin Goziem Jireh and Ingrid Harris, PhD

Exegesis is the interpretation of a text by way of a thorough analysis of its content in order to clarify its meaning. Our main task in exegesis is to discover the original, intended meaning of a given text through careful, systematic study. It is the process of examining a text to ascertain what its first readers would have understood it to mean.

And, based on the foregoing statement, we cannot agree with scholars who say that exegesis is an effort at reaching back into history to the original author and audience. To do a successful exegesis therefore, a person needs to apply grammatical, lexicographical, and structural tools to "discover" the author's original intended meaning in a given test. Thus, one must have a good translation, a good Bible dictionary, and good commentaries in order to do a good exegetical job. The most important thing a person should do in exegesis is to determine the original message of the author in order to understand the word of God for our modern context, that is to say, you must first understand the word of God for its ancient context.

Hermeneutics, on the other hand, is defined as the study of the locus of meaning and the principles of interpretation. It is concerned with the philosophy and science of interpretation. A Christian commentator once said. "Hermeneutics are a type of discernment process, ways of mining for God and God's truth. We're exploring what is endless and beyond our ability to comprehend."

According to Dakes, Scripture shows there are "nine (9)[8] ways the Bible was given through:

1. Audible voice of God (Exodus 19:19; Matthew 3:16-17)
2. Angels (Acts 7:38; Hebrews 2:2)
3. Prophets (Acts 3;21 Hebrews 1:1)
4. Jesus Christ (Hebrews 1:1; Revelation 1)

---

8 Dakes page 420

5. Apostles (Acts 1:2; Ephesians. 4)
6. Visions (Isaiah 6; Daniel7:8)
7. Dreams (Daniel 2; Matthew 1:20)
8. Revelation (Revelation 1:7; 2:2)
9. Inspiration (2 Timothy. 3:15-17)

2 Timothy 3:15 - *And that from a child thou hast known the holy scriptures, which are able to make thee wise unto salvation through faith which is in Christ Jesus.*

2 Timothy 3:16 - *All scripture is given by inspiration of God and is profitable for doctrine, for reproof, for correction, for instruction in righteousness;*

2 Timothy 3:17 - *That the man of God may be perfect, thoroughly furnished unto all good works.*

2 Peter 1:20 - *Knowing this first, that no prophecy of the scripture is of any private interpretation.*

2 Peter 1:21 - *For the prophecy came not in old time by the will of man; but holy men of God spake as they were moved by the Holy Ghost.*

While having some knowledge of the principles of exegesis and hermeneutics can be a useful tool in getting a better understanding of the Trinity, they are not necessary. The Bible is written in a manner than both adults and children are able to learn about God and develop a personal relationship with Him. However, application of those principles will allow the reader to seek out the truths of the Bible with confidence. Once those truths have been discovered, the reader can enjoy a more fruitful and life-changing existence.

RIGHTLY DIVIDING THE WORD OF TRUTH

2 Timothy 2:15 states:

> *Study to shew thyself approved unto God, a workman that needeth not to be ashamed, rightly dividing the word of truth.*

This scripture deals with someone (workman) as being one who is walking in righteousness according to the Word of God; is a servant of Christ and filled with the Holy Spirit. His works are acceptable and approved by God and by those qualified to know the characteristics of one who walks in an orderly manner. This workman or laborer is one who will give a straight and accurate meaning or account of the scripture along with the correct application. They will not deviate from the true intention or meaning the writer is trying to communicate.

One example of "rightly dividing the word of truth" has to do with the interpretation of the King James Version of Hosea 4:6. It was directed to the people of Israel because of the failure of the priests among them. Both the priest and the people gave in to temptation and ceased to acknowledge God. In today's context, it still applies and hopefully the following will present a simplified outline of this scripture that is more easily understood:

> **Hosea 4:6** - *My people are destroyed for lack of knowledge: because thou hast rejected knowledge, I will also reject thee, that thou shalt be no priest to me: seeing thou hast forgotten the law of thy God, I will also forget thy children.*

1. Who are these individuals called "my people" that are in jeopardy of being destroyed?

It is imperative that the interpretation of this passage is not taken out of context as it relates to the people of Israel and the failure of the priest to perform their assignment. According to 1 Peter 2:5-10, Christians are the priest today which is substantiated in the following verses:

1Peter 2:5 - *Ye also, as lively stones, are built up a spiritual house, an holy priesthood, to offer up spiritual sacrifices, acceptable to God by Jesus Christ.*

1Peter 2:6 - *Wherefore also it is contained in the scripture, Behold, I lay in Sion a chief cornerstone, elect, precious, and he that believeth on him shall not be confounded.*

1Peter 2:7 - *Unto you therefore which believe he is precious: but unto them which be disobedient, the stone which the builders disallowed, the same is made the head of the corner,*

1Peter 2:8 - *And a stone of stumbling, and a rock of offence, even to them which stumble at the word, being disobedient: whereunto also they were appointed.*

1Peter 2:9 - *But ye are a chosen generation, a royal priesthood, an holy nation, a peculiar people, that ye should shew forth the praises of him who hath called you out of darkness into his marvelous light:*

1Peter 2:10 - *Which in time past were not a people but are now the people of God; which had not obtained mercy, but now have obtained mercy.*

God promised He would write His laws in our hearts, and the Spirit would bring back to our remembrance all things we have heard and learned. God's people today are led by the Spirit of God as described in Galatians 4:6-7:

Galatians 4:6 - *And because ye are sons, God hath sent forth the Spirit of his Son into your hearts, crying, Abba, Father.*

Galatians 4:7 - *Wherefore thou art no more a servant, but a son; and if a son, then an heir of God through Christ.*

2. How does "lack of knowledge" lead to destruction?

According to Isaiah 5:13:

Therefore, my people are gone into captivity, because they have no knowledge: and their honourable men are famished, and their multitude dried up with thirst.

And *Proverbs 1:27-31*:

Proverbs 1:27 - *When your fear cometh as desolation, and your destruction cometh as a whirlwind; when distress and anguish cometh upon you.*

Proverbs 1:28 - *Then shall they call upon me, but I will not answer they shall seek me early, but they shall not find me:*

Proverbs 1:29 - *For that they hated knowledge, and did not choose the fear of the Lord:*

Proverbs 1:30 - *They would none of my counsel: they despised all my reproof.*

Proverbs 1:31 - *Therefore shall they eat of the fruit of their own way, and be filled with their own devices.*

Ephesians 4 addresses the issue in this way:

Ephesians 4:17 - *This I say therefore, and testify in the Lord, that ye henceforth walk not as other Gentiles, walk, in the vanity of their mind.*

Ephesians 4:18 - *Having the understanding darkened, being alienated from the life of God through the ignorance that is in them, because of the blindness of their heart?*

Ephesians 4:19 - *Who being past feeling have given themselves over unto lasciviousness, to work all uncleanness with greediness.*

Acts 17:30 gives warning to those who continue to plead ignorant and/or assume "what you don't know won't hurt you:

And the times of this ignorance God winked at; but now commandeth all men every where to repent.

3. How are God's people able to receive knowledge?

Ephesians 3:

Ephesians 3:1 - *For this cause, I Paul, the prisoner of Jesus Christ for you Gentiles,*

Ephesians 3:2 - *If ye have heard of the dispensation of the grace of God which is given me to you ward:*

Ephesians 3:3 - *How that by revelation he made known unto me the mystery (as I wrote afore in few words,*

Ephesians 3:4 - *Whereby, when ye read, ye may understand my knowledge in the mystery of Christ).*

2 Peter 3:18 - *But grow in grace, and in the knowledge of our Lord and Saviour Jesus Christ. To him be glory both now and for ever. Amen.*

1 Peter 2:2 - *As newborn babes, desire the sincere milk of the word, that ye may grow thereby.*

Our desire should be to serve a God who is able to do anything but fail. He would not set us out on a journey without providing a road map on how to follow it. He would not withhold access to His plan and then punish us for not following it. It is through the written word of God that we are able to obtain the knowledge we need to live a full and abundant life.

The Bible provides an opportunity to grow in knowledge and spiritually.

Ephesians 1:13 - *In whom ye also trusted, after that ye heard the word of truth, the gospel of your salvation, in whom also, after that ye believed, ye were sealed with that holy Spirit of promise,*

Ephesians 1:14 - *Which is the earnest of our inheritance until the redemption of the purchased possession unto the praise of his glory.*

Once we have gained and applied this knowledge, through reading and studying God's word, and by faith, it becomes wisdom when effectively and accurately used on a daily basis, thus giving us access to the Kingdom of Heaven.

CHAPTER 2
THE TRINITY

THE TRINITY CONSIST OF THREE PERSONS

"The names, titles and offices of the Father, the Son, and the Holy Ghost, reveal their character, work, and the individual parts in the plan of God that are being carried out by the THREE separate and distinct persons of the Trinity.

There are several scriptures in the Bible that give reference to how God's plan includes all three members of the Trinity. God the Father designed and organized how mankind would be redeemed Galatians 4:4-5. He set into motion a complex set of events, actions, and prophecies which culminated in the life and death of a Savior. The Son carried out the plan John 6:37-38. He followed the Father's instructions to come to earth, even though that meant He would have to die. The Holy Spirit sees to it that every person feels a call toward God's saving grace John 14:26, John 16:8; Romans 1:19-20. Furthermore, the Spirit transforms the lives and hearts of those who receive salvation through Jesus Christ.

The Father, Son, and Spirit are equal in their divine attributes. Yet each relates to mankind in a different way because each one has a specific role. It's very important to understand this distinction. We do not have three Gods; we have one God in three persons functioning uniquely and perfectly."[9]

WHY WE SHOULD UNDERSTAND THE TRINITY?

To understand the Trinity is to understand God and how relevant it is for us to know His thoughts and His will for us. Since we know we are made in His image, it should be of the utmost importance to know how, individually, we fit into the overall creation of the universe.

To seek further knowledge about God will ultimately lead to a better understanding and insight into the "fearfully and wonderfully made" person He has made each one of us to be.

When it comes to learning any and everything we can about each person of the Trinity, we should know it matters to God how we view Him. John 3:16 says:

> *For God so loved the world, that he gave his only begotten Son, that whosoever believeth in him should not perish, but have everlasting life.*

This scripture is relevant because God views himself as "our Father" and wants us to understand that concept. He wants to care for us and provide us with all the benefits He intends for us to have. The fact that the Father gave his Son tells us they are two distinct persons. The Father can't be the Son if he gave the Son. It shows the first two persons of the Trinity. It demonstrates the love He has for us as sinners. To give His ONLY Son is the ultimate sacrifice for God. The Son of God becomes a Son of Man, so that the sons of men might become sons of God. Then, the Father (first person) and Son (Jesus Christ and second person) sent their Spirit (third person) to dwell within us.

---

9 Charles Stanley

The Trinity matters because God matters. To understand God's intended purpose for us will determine the kind of relationship we have with Him.

GOD'S IMAGE AND THE TRINITY

While there may be repetition of some scripture, the purpose is solely for the clarification of a specific idea. One instance is in repeating

> **Genesis 1:26** - *And God said, Let us make man in our image, after our likeness:*

> **Genesis 1:27** - *So God created man in his own image, in the image of God created he him; male and female created he them.*

It is in this scripture where God establishes the Trinity. The "us" and "our" is plural, and thus means more than one.

MAN MADE IN THE IMAGE OF GOD FOR A PURPOSE

Since we can't see God, we can experience God in a spiritual sense. What makes up the spiritual aspects or characteristics of God. In Genesis 1:27, when God made man in His image, that implies that the characteristics of man must meet specific standards. Those standards should, in some way, compare to the uniqueness of the "us" and "our" of God.

> **Exodus 31:3** - *And I have filled him with the spirit of God, in wisdom, and in understanding, and in knowledge, and in all manner of workmanship.*

Knowledge, understanding, and wisdom are a few of the characteristics that man was endowed with as God the Father, God the Son and God the Holy Spirit proceeded to ensure man's image reflected that of God. A person who possesses knowledge, must have the capability to accomplish complex assignments.

To demonstrate understanding, man must be able to display his talent or gift to understand the process of production. A person with wisdom has the intellect to know the difference between right and wrong.

Man's image would also have to reflect the fruit of the Spirit as outlined in

> **Galatians 5:22-23** - *But the fruit of the Spirit is love, joy, peace, longsuffering, gentleness, goodness, faith, meekness, temperance: against such there is no law*

CHAPTER 3

GOD THE FATHER

SCRIPTURE REVEALS THE FATHER HOLDS THE OFFICE OF HEADSHIP

Headship means that one who has assumed the position or office as head or chief. As a supreme being, God is the ultimate head and only authority to whom everyone else reports. *Merriam-Webster* gives the definition as—"the position, office, or dignity of a head." Various synonyms for headship are care, charge, guidance, oversight, regulation, stewardship, superintendence, supervision and surveillance.

Cambridge Dictionary gives headship definition as "being the position of being in charge of an organization." A list of synonyms or related words include dean, handler, headteacher, instructor, mentor, professorship, scribe, trainer, tutor, and many more.

WHERE DID GOD COME FROM AND WHERE IS GOD NOW

God is defined in simple terms as being the Eternal, the Infinite Spirit, Creator, Redeemer, Sovereign Lord:

Genesis 1:1 - *In the beginning God created the heaven and the earth.*

God has always existed.

Psalm 8:3 - *When I consider thy heavens, the work of thy fingers; the moon and the stars, which thou hast ordained.*

John 1:3 - *All things were made by him; and without him was not any thing made that was made.*

Psalm 115:2 - *Wherefore should the heathens say, Where is now their God?*

Psalm 115:3 - *But our God is in the heavens, he hath done whatsoever he hath pleased.*

These scriptures establish God as the maker of the heavens and the earth which include the entire solar system. That also includes the sun and moon, all planets and stars.

Psalm 115:2 - *Wherefore should the heathens say, Where is now their God?*

Psalm 115:3 - *But our God is in the heavens, he hath done whatsoever he hath pleased.*

These scriptures are a reference to a prayer of Moses who acknowledges that God was there from the beginning of time and considered to be the eternal God with no beginning and no ending.

Isaiah 48: 16 - *Come ye near unto me, hear ye this; I have not spoken in secret from the beginning; from the time that it was, there am I: and now the Lord GOD, and his Spirit, hath sent me.*

This scripture describes one of the best examples of the Trinity as the Messiah is sent to appeal to Israel. He was sent by God and His Spirit. It speaks to the Lord God (one person) the Holy Spirit (another person) and the Messiah (still another person):

Psalm 90:1-2 - *Lord, thou hast been our dwelling place in all generations. Before the mountains were brought forth, or ever thou hadst formed the earth and the word, even from everlasting to everlasting, thou art God.*

Job 36:26 - *Behold, God is great, and we know him not, neither can the number of his years be searched out,*

Colossians 1:16 - *For by him were all things created, that are in heaven, and that are in earth, visible and invisible, whether they be thrones, dominions, or principalities, or powers, all things were created.*

Hebrews 13:8 - *Jesus Christ the same yesterday, and today, and forever.*

Revelation 1:8 - *I am Alpha and Omega, the beginning and the ending, saith the Lord, which is, and which was, and which is to come, the Almighty.*

Galatians 4:4-5 - *But when the fulness of the time was come, God sent forth his Son, made of a woman, made under the law. To redeem them that were under the law, that we might receive the adoption of sons.*

Romans 11:33 - *O the depth of the riches both of the wisdom and knowledge of God! How unsearchable are his judgments, and his ways past finding out!*

Romans 11:34 - *For who hath known the mind of the Lord? Or who hath been his counselor?*

Romans 11:35 - *Or who hath first given to him, and it shall be recompensed unto him again?*

Romans 11:36 - *For of him, and through him, and to him are all things: to whom be glory forever.*

These scriptures tell us He is the beginning and the end, and the First and the Last.

The ***Eternal*** God of the Bible who has always existed and will always exist. Described as being the one who existed before the mountains were born; who is timeless and has no beginning or end. Job describes God as being beyond our understanding, and his years are too many to count, and extend beyond where we can go. Col 1:16 tells us that even time and space did not exist before the creation of the universe. His ***Infinite Spirit***—meaning God has no limits. The ***Creator*** who has wisdom and power that never end. The ***Redeemer*** who gives evidence through the sacrifice of His son Jesus Christ that we might be delivered from physical or spiritual bondage.

Romans 11:33-36 describes a Sovereign God who knows all things from past to the present and the future to come. God is defined in simple terms as being eternal, the infinite Spirit, Creator, Redeemer, sovereign Lord.

This passage in Genesis shows God referring to Himself as "Us":

Genesis 1:26 - *And God Said, Let us make man in our image, after our likeness: and let them have dominion over the fish of the sea, and over the foul of the air, and over the cattle, and over all the earth, and over every creeping thing that creepeth upon the earth.*

In Genesis 1:26 we see this is the first referencing of the Trinity as God the Father, God the Son, and God the Holy Spirit.

God establishes the Trinity when He uses the nouns "us" and "our" which denotes more than one. God is referring to the creation of man being made in "their" image with all the characteristics and attributes that God possesses. God establishes in those two verses that there was more than one.

John 1:1 says In the beginning was the Word, and the Word was with God, and the Word was God. This scripture establishes that from the very beginning, which is the same beginning mentioned in Gen. 1:1; God the Father already and always existed. The Word refers to Jesus Christ His Son, and the Holy Spirit. These are two of my favorite scriptures that gives clarity to the following:

The **Living Word r**efers to God the Father and God the Son.
The **Spoken Word** refers to the Gospel of Jesus Christ or God the Son.
The **Written Word** refers to the Bible or the Holy Scriptures.

CHARACTERISTICS OF GOD

The characteristics of God are described in several scriptures. Five of those characteristics can be found in Numbers 14.

Numbers 14:17 - *And now, I beseech thee, let the power of my LORD be great, according as thou has spoken, saying,*

Numbers 14:18 - *The LORD is longsuffering and of great mercy, forgiving iniquity and transgression, and by no means clearing the guilty, visiting the iniquity of the fathers upon the children unto the third and fourth generation.*

Numbers 14:19 - *Pardon, I beseech thee, the iniquity of this people according unto the greatness of thy mercy, and as thou hast forgiven this people, from Egypt even until now.*

Numbers 14:20 - *And the LORD said, I have pardoned according to thy word.*

These characteristics are mentioned as Moses appealed to God's love, His mercy and His promises. God's character must not be questioned. There must be confirmation at all times. His plan must be accomplished to the end.

The Book of Numbers 14:18 *Dake's Annotated Reference Bible,* June 2000) give descriptive definitions of God characteristics: The Lord *is* longsuffering and of great mercy, forgiving iniquity and transgression, and by no means clearing *the guilty*, visiting the iniquity of the fathers upon the children unto the third and fourth *generation.*

While I found that scripture comforting, it serves as an ominous admonition that although God does forgive when we confess our sins, He warns us not to return back to those sinful ways. However, if we do continue in sin, His longsuffering, His mercy and His love will not let Him bestow blessings on men while they continue to be disobedient. In addition, we could be responsible for our future generations to receive punishment for our iniquities.

Psalms 36:5-8 also clearly defines the characteristics of God in the following order:

Psalm 36:5 - *Thy* ***mercy****, O LORD, is in the heavens; and thy faithfulness reacheth unto the clouds.*

Psalm 36:6 - *Thy* ***righteousness*** *is like the great mountains;* ***thy judgments*** *are a great deep: O LORD,* ***thou preservest*** *man and beast.*

Psalm 36: 7 - *How excellent is thy* ***lovingkindness****, O God! Therefore, the children of men put their trust under the shadow of thy wings.*

Psalm 36:8 - *They shall be* ***abundantly satisfied*** *with the fatness of thy house; and* ***thou shalt*** *make them drink of the river of thy pleasures.*

Psalm 36:9 - *For with thee is the* ***fountain of life: in thy light shall we see light****.*

Characteristics in Psalms 36 address ten (10) of the attributes of God in the following order:

1. Mercy – extends into the heavens
2. Faithfulness – reaches into the cloud
3. Righteousness – exceeds the highest mountain
4. Justice – deep as the abyss
5. Preservation – keeps both man and beast
6. Kindness – so excellent we put our trust in you
7. Providence – we shall be completely satisfied
8. Satisfaction – rivers of pleasure
9. Life – the fountain of life
10. Light – source of truth

WHY WE NEED DAILY CONTACT WITH GOD

The Lord's Prayer can be found in Luke Chapter 11:1-4, where one of his disciples asked Jesus to teach them how to pray. In verse 3, he said *"Give us day by day our daily bread."* In this scripture, Jesus instructs us that we should have "daily bread" which is to say we need to be nourished by His Word every day. There are seven times that Luke references Jesus praying. In Luke 3:21-22,

Luke makes mention of Jesus praying as He is baptized. It is also in verse 22 where the Trinity is mentioned. This verse gives a definitive look into three (3) separate and distinct persons:

> **Luke 3: 22** - *And the Holy Ghost descended in a bodily shape like a dove upon him, and a voice came from heaven, which said, Thou art my beloved Son, in thee I am well pleased.*

In this verse, our heavenly Father (God) spoke from Heaven, as the Son (our Lord and Savior Jesus Christ) was here on earth praying to the Father who was in heaven. And at the same time, The Holy Spirit, in the form of a dove, descended from His place in heaven where God the Father resides. The purpose of the Holy Spirit (dove) was to anoint and confer power to the Son of God to exercise and walk in that power while He was here on earth.

WE CANNOT COMPREHEND HIM (GOD) BY HUMAN EFFORT-1 CORINTHIANS 2:15-16

According to scripture, the natural man is living according to his/her fleshly passions. That is in reference to the animal man and not the spiritual man. The natural man is not able to comprehend or understand God by human effort. The natural man cannot understand the things of the Spirit. God can only be understood through the spiritual man; one who has been born again of the Spirit. Because the Spirit man lives according to the Holy Spirit, he has the mind of Christ and thus is able to discern the spiritual things of God. The spiritual man is able to resist the carnal things of life.

HOW GOD COMMUNICATES WITH US

It is documented through Scripture that God communicates with man in various ways. It is recorded in:

1. Daniel 7:9-14: to give clarity to what the people of God would experience the magnificent coming of Christ, the destruction of the antichrist and establish His own kingdom on earth.
2. Daniel 2:28: God communicated to man **through dreams and visions**.
3. John 3:16: God **sent His own Son Jesus Christ** for those that believed on Him would have eternal life.
4. John 16:7: He **sent the Holy Spirit** to the believers.
5. Hebrews 1:14: God **sent ministering angels** to care for the people.
6. Acts 3:21: God **sent His prophets** to speak during the ancient times.
7. 2Timothy 3:16-17, God provides guidance, lessons and instruction **through His Word** in Scripture.

UNDERSTANDING THE HEART OF GOD

The purpose of this section will provide a teaching tool for any and all on this complex subject matter. You will be able to connect the dots quickly and definitively without losing continuity of God's overall plan.

To fully understand God, you need to know what is in the Heart of God. Having a good understanding of His heart, will allow you to see a little deeper into the things of God and how His plan is intended to work in your favor. As the Creator of man, God has our welfare before Him at all times. He has always wanted what is best for us. His plan that comes from His heart will get us to where we need to be in life. To oppose His plan, will only delay the blessings He has in store for you.

God not only makes Himself known through the Scriptures, but also reveals what we can expect from Him, as well as what He expects from us.

Genesis 3:9 is a great example of His loving care as a Father. After Adam and Eve had disobeyed God and hid themselves, God asked, "where are you?"

One of the characteristics of a father is to reach out to his children. He wants to know what we're doing, to verify that all in well with us. Because God is concerned about our relationship with Him, He will come looking for us. God the Son also has a passion to stay in a relationship with us. Even if we are the one who has broken the relationship with Him. But like His Father, Jesus has a heart that seeks to keep us close.

The Great Commission of Matthew. 28:19, Jesus commands us to *"Go ye, therefore, and teach all nations, baptizing them in the name of the Father, and of the Son, and of the Holy Ghost."* This is our charge to imitate God the Father and God the Son, by seeking out others to be a witness to the goodness and mercy of God, and ultimately bringing them into the fold as well. In our commission, we are asking the question, "where are you?" to those who are lost, backslidden or have not received salvation. Salvation means to accept Jesus Christ, by faith, into ones heart, as Lord and Savior. The unbeliever's acceptance of Christ begins the framework for the Christian walk.

The paragraph above reminded me of a recent sermon my pastor, Dr. Fred L. Hodge, Jr. delivered in March 2019, at Living Praise Christian Center (LPCC) Palmdale, California.

The sermon preached on that Sunday was among many that I have heard, and also serve as an inspiration for this book. That specific sermon referenced Genesis 8:1, *"And God remembered Noah."* The question "where are you?" as an individual, caused me to reflect on myself and others. The thought came to me, how can I be sure that God knows me, how can I be sure that He remembers me? I am reassured when I read this scripture that God does know my name, that He does remember me, because I've had a lifetime of sending up prayers and petitions. He does remember me by name because of the personal relationship and spiritual encounters I've had with Him for many years. I've always endeavored to seek more and more knowledge concerning the things of

God. But what about others whose walk in life or their relationship with God has not been the same as mine.

I feel it's incumbent upon me to do my part to encourage others to acknowledge Him, pray to Him, thank Him, petition Him, esteem Him, extol Him, lift Him up at all times. The only way to do this is to know as much about Him as you can. So, that when you go to Him in prayer, it's an honest, earnest prayer or petition because you know who He is, and what He's capable of performing on your behalf. I've concluded we all need to give God a reason to remember us by name as He remembered Noah.

According to Dakes, there are several people God Remembers in the Bible, but to mention a few:

Genesis 8:1: **God remembered Noah** and caused the flood to cease.

Genesis18:23 and 19:29: **God remembered Abraham** who prayed and asked God if He would destroy the righteous along with the wicked concerning Sodom and Gomorrah. God spared Lot on Abraham's behalf.

Genesis 30:22: **God remembered Rachel** when He saw she was in turmoil because of being barren and not able to bear a child. God opened her womb, and she was able to conceive.

1 Samuel 1:8: **God remembered Hannah**. Hannah had reason to cry out to God for an answer as to why her womb had been closed. She knew that the path to motherhood also equated to her womanhood and being without child she felt less than. But her prayers did not fall on deaf ears when she vowed to God, and through her prayer and supplication, would dedicate her child back to Him. God answered Hannah when she became pregnant with Samuel.

As an ordained minister since 1993, I feel this was my reasonable service. To communicate what God has given me to share with others. To minister wherever to whoever, so they do not perish. I want to be sure that God remembers me.

Because God remembers those who are faithful to Him, we should also remember Him as the God who is called Jehovah by the Hebrews. The following represent some of the names the Hebrews knew God as:

GOD JEHOVAH

Jehovah-Jireh – The **Lord will see or provide** in Genesis 22:8-14 where God told Abraham to offer his son Isaiah as a burn offering. This was a place in the land of Moriah, the location of the binding of Isaiah where Abraham was willing to sacrifice his son. Abraham named the place after God provided a ram to sacrifice in place of Isaiah.

Jehovah-Nissi – Hebrews name also known as the **Lord our banner**; a name given by Moses in Exodus 17:14-16 for the altar that he built to celebrate the defeat of the Amalekites.

Jehovah-Rapha – Hebrews name for **Lord my Healer** in Exodus 15:26 where God revealed himself as Jehovah the Healer or the Physician that is able to heal you physically, emotionally and spiritually.

Jehovah-Shalom – Hebrews for **Lord our Peace** in Judges 6:23-24 where an angel of the Lord came to Gideon and said, *"Peace be unto thee, fear not; thou shalt not die."* And Gideon built an altar there unto the Lord and called it Jehovah-Shalom which according to scripture is located at Ophrah of the Abiezrites. The word meaning peace, completeness, harmony, wholeness, prosperity, welfare and tranquility.

Jehovah-Tsidqenuw – *Jeremiah 23:6 - In his days Judah shall be saved, and Israel shall dwell safely; and this is his name whereby he shall be called* ***THE LORD OUR RIGHTEOUSNESS****, which is the title given to the Messiah.*

Jehovah-Mekaddishkem – English translation of the Hebrew word for "I am the Lord which sanctify you, taken from Leviticus 20:7-8 as He commanded "Sanctify yourselves therefore, and be ye holy: for I am the LORD your God. And ye shall keep my statutes and do them: **I am the LORD which sanctify you**.

Jehovah—Sabaoth – The **Lord of hosts**, Hebrew word meaning heavenly host in Luke 2:13; And suddenly there was with the angel a **multitude of the heavenly host praising God** and saying, Glory to God in the highest, and on earth peace, good will toward men.

Jehovah-Shammah – The Lord is present (or there) as in Ezekiel 48:35 "It was round about eighteen thousand measures; and the name of the city from that day shall be **The LORD is there**. A reference to Jerusalem, it is one of fourteen (14) names for Jerusalem.

Jehovah-Elyown – As in Psalm 7:17 "I will praise the LORD according to his righteousness: and will sing praise to the name of the **LORD most high**."

Jehovah-Rohi – Hebrew word meaning shepherd as in Psalms 23:1 "**The LORD is my shepherd:** I shall not want. Both the Old and New Testaments teach that lawful wants and needs will be supplied.

Jehovah-Hoseenu – as in Psalm 95:6 "O come, let us worship and bow down; let us kneel before the **LORD our maker**. Where Elohim shows us how God creates out of nothing, Hoseenu shows us how God moulds it and shapes it (Adam and Eve).

Jehovah-Eloheka – as in Exodus 20:2 "I am the **LORD thy God**, which have brought thee out of the land of Egypt, out of the house of bondage.

Jehovah-Elohay – the Lord my God as in Psalms 91:1-2 "He that dwelleth in the secret place of the Highest shall abide under the shadow of the Almighty. I will say of the LORD, He is my refuge and my fortress: my God: in him will I trust."

Psalms 91, I believe, is one of the most effective scriptures in which to identify. Every verse seems to present a place where I can insert my name and see a personal need to call upon the **Lord My God**. This should be a fairly easy scripture to read, digest, meditate on, and make it a personal dedication. It is one where you can focus, read over and over until there is revelation into just how great God is and can be.

CHAPTER 4

GOD THE SON, JESUS CHRIST

JESUS CHRIST HAS THE CREATIVE AND REDEMPTIVE OFFICES

In keeping to Scripture that reveals all three persons of the Trinity are God with separate and distinctions parts. To fully understand Jesus Christ the second person of the Trinity and His characteristics, we find those in the following verses:

> **John 1:1** - *In the beginning was the Word (God), and the Word was with God (Jesus Christ), and the Word was God (Holy Spirit).*
>
> **John 1:2** - *The same was in the beginning with God*
>
> **John 1:3** - *All things were made by him, and without him was not anything made that was made.*

As Christ, the offices held by Jesus are that of Prophet, Priest and King. The execution of these three offices are essential to the salvation of God's people. It is critical that we know the substance of these offices, what they mean and how they apply to the life of the believer and/or those who seek to become Christian. **Christ as Prophet:** As prophet, Jesus delivers the Word of God to sinful people; and yet is faithful to obey His Father's Word for the benefit of the people.

> **John 17:8** - *For I have given unto them the words which thou gavest me; and they have received them and have known surely that I came out froms thee, and they have believed that thou didst send me.*

> **Hebrews 5:8** - *Though he were a Son yet learned he obedience by the things which he suffered.*

Christ as Priest: Although Jesus Christ is holy and blameless, He is still able to understand the frailties of man. And because of his love for His Father, he is able to mediate and intercede on our behalf. His office of priesthood is the basis for the priesthood of all believers who chose Him and make our own spiritual sacrifices.

> **Romans 12:1** - *I beseech you therefore, brethren, by the mercies of God, that ye present your bodies a living sacrifice, holy acceptable unto God which is; your reasonable service.*

> **1 Peter 2:5** - *Ye also, as lively stones, are built up a spiritual house, an holy priesthood, to offer up spiritual sacrifices, acceptable to God by Jesus Christ.*

> **Romans 8:34** - *Who is he that condemneth? It is Christ that died, yea rather, that is risen again, who is even at the right hand of God, who also maketh intercession for us.*

Hebrews 7:25 - *Wherefore he is able to save them to the uttermost that come unto God by him, seeing he ever liveth to make intercession for them.*

Romans 12:1 maintains *"this is our reasonable service"* for the sacrifice Jesus made for us. To give His life that we might have a right to the Tree of Life. God is not asking for anything "extra" but only that which is reasonable.

Christ as King: With the death, burial and resurrection of Christ, Jesus became King of kings and Lord of lords. His victory establishes His power and glory, righteousness to execute authority and judgment over all the earth.

2 Timothy 4:1 - *I charge thee therefore before God, and the Lord Jesus Christ, who shall judge the quick and the dead, at his appearing and his kingdom;*

2 Timothy 4:2 - *Preach the word, be instant in season, out of season; reprove, rebuke, exhort with all longsuffering and doctrine.*

CHARACTERISTICS OF JESUS

There are many qualities of Jesus Christ through scripture that highlight his moral character as follows:

Charity – When we love one another we reflect God's love for us.

1Corinthiansithians 13: 4 - *Charity suffereth long and is kind; charity envieth not; charity vaunteth not itself, is not puffed up.*

Compassion – Show sympathy, concern for, and a willingness to help others.

Ephesians 4:32 - *And be ye kind one to another, tenderhearted, forgiving one another, even as God for Christ's sake hath forgiven you.*

Endurance – Maintain strength in the face of adversity without giving up.

Hebrews 12:2 - *Looking unto Jesus the author and finisher of our faith, who for the joy that was set before him endured the cross, despising the shame, and is set down at the right hand of the throne of God*

Faithful – Stay loyal, be steadfast, unmovable, have confidence in things to come.

Hebrews 11:1 - *Now faith, is the substance of things hoped for, the evidence of things not seen.*

Forgiveness – A deliberate decision to release feelings of resentment or vengeance toward a person or group who has harmed you.

Colossians 3:13 - *Forbearing one another, and forgiving one another, if any man have a quarrel against any: even Christ forgave you, so also do ye,*

Generous/Giving – That our service is to keep our eyes and hearts open to the need of others.

2 Corinthians 9:6 - *But this I say, He which soweth sparingly shall reap also sparingly; and he which soweth bountifully shall reap also bountifully.*

Holiness – Walk orderly keeping the things of God before you as sacred and pure.

1 Peter 1:15 - *But as he which hath called you is holy, so be ye holy in all manner of conversation;*

1 Peter 1: 16 - *Because it is written, Be ye holy, for I am holy.*

Humble - Be not proud, be submissive to the divine will of God.

1 Peter 5:6 - *Humble yourselves therefore under the mighty hand of God, that he may exalt you in due time.*

Humility – Be comfortable in God, don't display pride and arrogance.

Philippians 2:3 - *Let nothing be done through strife or vainglory, but in lowliness of mind let each esteem other better than themselves.*

Kindness – Show good will and benevolence, be charitable and hospitality.

Luke 6:35 - *But love yet your enemies, and do good and lend hoping for nothing again, and your reward shall be great, and ye shall be the children of the Highest, for he is kind unto the unthankful and to the evil.*

Love – Love is patient, love is kind, love demonstrates what the human heart has to offer.

1 Corinthians 13:5 - *Doth not behave itself unseemly, seeketh not her own, is not easily provoked, thinketh no evil:*

1 Corinthians 13:6 - *Rejoiceth not in iniquity, but rejoiceth in the truth*

1 Corinthians 13:7 - *Beareth all things, believeth all things, hopeth all things, endureth all things.*

Obedience – Be submissive to authority, trust in the knowledge of God and His statutes.

John 15:10 - *If ye keep my commandments, ye shall abide in my love; even as I have kept my Father's commandments and abide in his love.*

Patient – Be kind to one another as we bear offenses without anger or revenge.

Romans 5:3 - *And not only so, but we glory in tribulations also: knowing that tribulations worketh patience;*

Romans 5:4 - *And patience, experience; and experience, hope:*

Romans 5:5 - *And hope maketh not ashamed, because the love of God is shed abroad in our hearts by the Holy Ghost which is given unto us.*

Prayerful – Pray often keeping all things before God, allow prayer to be a way of life.

Romans 1:9 - *For God is my witness, whom I serve with my spirit in the gospel of his Son, that without ceasing I make mention of you always in my prayers.*

Purity – Refrain from any sinister or impure views, motives or designs.

1John 3:3 - *And every man that hath this hope in him purifieth himself, even as he is pure.*

Righteousness – One of the main attributes of God concerning integrity and ethical conduct.

> **Psalm 1:6** - *For the Lord knoweth the way of the righteous: but the way of the ungodly shall perish.*

Submission – Be subject to one another for the sake of peace within the body of Christ.

> **Ephesians 5:21** - *Submitting yourselves one to another in the fear of God.*

Wise – Increase in wisdom as we grow in the Word of God, judging correctly.

> **2Timothy 3:16** - *All scripture is given by inspiration of God, and is profitable for doctrine for reproof, for correction, for instruction in righteousness:*

> **2Timothy 3:17** - *That the man of God may be perfect, thoroughly furnished unto all good works.*

Virtuous – Turn away from those things that poison our minds, bodies and spirits.

> **Philippians 4:8** - *Finally brethren, whatsoever things are true, whatsoever things are honest, whatsoever things are just, whatsoever things are pure, whatsoever things are lovely, whatsoever things are of good report; if there be any virtue, and if there be any praise, think on those things.*

These characteristics of Jesus are but a few of all that He possessed in His brief walk on this earth. He sent the Spirit to strengthen us, to empower us to be sure that we, too, could walk in those characteristics.

I compare other characteristics that Jesus possessed, as we should also, to that in *Galatians 5:22 - But the fruit of the Spirit is love, joy, peace, longsuffering, gentleness, goodness, faith,*

Galatians 5:23 - *Meekness, temperance, against such there is no law.*

According to scripture, when a believer walks in the fruit of the Spirit, no law can condemn them. Because law only condemns sin, it cannot condemn righteousness. Keeping in mind **ALL** the parts must be adhered to before that fruit is complete. As in the parts of an apple that comes with the leaves, stern or stem, flesh or pulp, core, seeds and skin. Those six parts make up the entire apple. Without any of those parts, the apple is flawed and may not be fit for consumption. A true Christian must endeavor to perfect their walk so that all the requirements of the fruit of the Spirit are met. A true Christian who is truly dedicated, will not perish.

Now that we have established that, according to the Bible, God is the first person of the Trinity, we'll go on to provide scripture references to Jesus Christ, the second person of the Trinity. Since the three are one, continue to follow along as I present the next few scriptures concerning God the Son. Apostle Paul while speaking to the Colossians, gives credit to how God the Son or Jesus Christ our Lord and Savior also existed from the beginning. Paul also ministers that no one can grow into Christ, but one can grow in wisdom and book knowledge. We learn and grow through our experiences, and from the grace and righteousness of being in Christ and walk according to his statutes.

In Luke 9:35, God clearly identifies Jesus as His Son:

Luke 9:35 - *And there came a voice out of the cloud, saying, This is my beloved Son: hear him.*

Luke 9: 36 - *And when the voice was past, Jesus was found alone. And they kept it close and told no man in those days any of those things which they had seen.*

Understanding Jesus is to understand God as reflected in Luke, Chapter 10 as expressed by Jesus:

Luke 10:22 - *All things are delivered to me of my Father: and no man knoweth who the Son is, but the Father; and who the Father is, but the Son, and he to whom the Son will reveal him.*

John records in Chapter 12 one of the last conversations Jesus had with the people. Jesus was quoted as saying:

John 12:44 - *Jesus cried and said, He that believeth on me, believeth not on me, but on him that sent me.*

John 12:45 - *And he that seeth me seeth him that sent me.*

The interpretation of the words Jesus spoke with passion, was to stress that those whose faith is in Christ, know also that to recognize Christ is to recognize the Father.

Jesus gives comfort to His disciples in John 14 after revealing that soon He was going away to prepare a place for them. Jesus in essence tells them that they know where He is going, and that they also know the way. Thomas answered saying we don't know where you're going, so how can we know the way. Philip, as well, sought answers, saying to the Savior, "show us the Father and we will be satisfied." Yet again, Jesus is asked to show them how He and the Father are one."

John 14:8 - *Philip saith unto him, Lord shew us the Father sufficeth and it sufficeth us.*

John 14:9 - *Jesus saith unto him, "Have I been so long time with you, and yet has thou not known me, Philip? He that hath seen me hath seen the Father; and how sayest thou then, Shew us the Father?*

John 14:10 - *Believeth thou not that I am in the Father and the Father in me? The words that I speak unto you I speak not of myself but the Father that dwelleth in me, he doeth the works.*

John 14:11 - *Believe me that I am in the Father, and the Father in me; or else believe me for the very works' sake.*

Colossians 1:12 - *Giving thanks unto the Father, which hath made us meet to be partakers of the inheritance of the saints in light;*

Colossians 1:13 - *Who hath delivered us from the power of darkness and hath translated us into the kingdom of his dear Son,*

Colossians 1:14 - *In whom we have redemption through his blood even the forgiveness of sins:*

Colossians 1:15 - *Who is the image of the invisible God the firstborn of every creature*

Colossians 1:16 - *For by him were all things created, that are in heaven and that are in earth, visible and invisible whether they be thrones or dominions or principalities, or powers: all things were created by him and for him.*

Colossians 1:17 - *And he is before all things, and by him all things consist.*

WHY JESUS CAME WHEN HE DID

Mark 1:1-2 explains why Jesus Christ, the Son of God, came:

Mark 1:1 - *The **beginning** of the gospel of Jesus Christ, the Son of God:*

Mark 1:2 - *As **it is written** in the prophets, Behold, I send my messenger before thy face, which shall prepare thy way before thee.*

Versus 1 and 2 address the ministry of John as a messenger of God that was the beginning of the gospel of the coming of the Messiah. John's assigned calling was to pave the way for the "coming" of Christ. The definition of "gospel" is "good news" or "glad tidings." Which is to expand and/or expound on the "message" and not so much on the "messenger." Although both have their own significance, John's ministry was to highlight the importance of the "living word" that later would become known as Jesus Christ.

WHEN JESUS ENTERED HISTORY

Matthew chapter 1 is the first of the gospels to give reference to the genealogy and the generations of Jesus Christ. While there are too many to outline here, Matthew 1:16 mentions the generations as follows:

Matthew 1:1 - *The book of the generation of Jesus Christ, the son of David, the son of Abraham.*

Matthew 1:17 - *So, all the generations from Abraham to David are fourteen generations, and from David until the carrying away into Babylon are fourteen generations; and from the carrying away into Babylon unto Christ are fourteen generations*

> **Matthew 1:18** - *Now the birth of Jesus Christ was on this wise: When as his mother Mary was espoused to Joseph, before they came together, she was found with child of the Holy Ghost.*

The interpretation of vs. 18 "*before they came together*" is that Joseph had not yet been intimate with Mary as she was still a virgin. And, conception of this child was the result of what is known as the "**immaculate conception**" of the Holy Ghost.

Both Mary and Joseph received visions and/or contact from an angel sent by God.

In Luke 1, it spells out the encounter between Mary and the angel Gabriel as it relates to her carrying the Messiah.

Mary: The visitation from the Angel Gabriel

> **Matthew 1:26** - *And in the sixth month the angel Gabriel was sent from God unto a city of Galilee named Nazareth.*

> **Matthew 1:27** - *To a virgin espoused to a man whose name was Joseph, of the house of David; and the virgin's name was Mary*

> **Matthew 1:28** - *And the angel came in unto her, and said, "Hail thou that art" highly favoured, the Lord is with thee; blessed art thou among women.*

Joseph: A vision from God

Matthew 1:20; 2:13

In the Gospel of Matthew, the scripture gives a look into the state of mind Joseph was in prior to a visitation from an angel of the Lord.

Matthew 1-20 - *But while he thought on these things, behold, the angel of the Lord appeared unto him in a dream, saying, Joseph, thou son of David, fear not to take unto thee Mary thy wife: for that which is conceived in her is of the Holy Ghost.*

Matthew 1:21 - *And she shall bring forth a son, and thou shalt call his name JESUS: for he shall save his people from their sins.*

Matthew 1:22 - *Now all this was done, that it might be fulfilled which was spoken of the Lord, by the prophet, saying,*

Matthew 1:23 - *Behold, a virgin shall be with child, and shall bring forth a son, and they shall call his name Emmanuel, which being interpreted is, God with us.*

Matthew 1:24 - *Then Joseph being raised from sleep did as the angel of the Lord had bidden him, and took unto him his wife:*

Matthew 1:25 - *And knew her not till she had brought forth her firstborn son: and he called his name JESUS.*

WHY THE VIRGIN BIRTH OF JESUS IS IMPORTANT

Belief in the doctrine of the Virgin Birth is of great significance among the body of Christ. It's either you believe ALL of the Bible or you believe NONE of it. The Four Gospels: Matthew, Mark, Luke and John address the historical events surrounding the birth and ministry of Jesus.

Don Stewart of *Blue Letter Bible Ministries*[10] give a fairly short synopsis of the importance of the Virgin Birth as follows:

---

10 Don Stewart, BBB

1. Jesus Had A Heavenly Origin

The most important reason to hold the belief in the Virgin Birth concerns Jesus' identity as God the Son, the Second Person of the Trinity.

In the beginning was the word, and the word was with God, and the word was God (John 1:1)

Thus, the virgin birth is crucial to Jesus being the Son of God.

2. Jesus Had a Sinless Nature

A second reason why the "virgin birth" is important, concerns the sinless character of Christ. If Jesus had a human father, then He would have inherited a sinful nature as the rest of us have. The Scripture states that Jesus never sinned.

And you know that he was manifested to take away our sins, and in him there is no sin (1 John 3:5).

3. Jesus as the Perfect Sacrifice

A third reason why the Virgin Birth is crucial to the Christian faith concerns our salvation.

For the Son of Man has come to seek and save that which was lost (Luke 19:10). God required a sacrifice that was without blemish.

Your lamb shall be without blemish (Exodus 12:5)

He came into the world by supernatural means and lived a sinless life.

For he made him who knew no sin to be sin for us, that we might become the righteousness of God in him (2Corinthiansinthians. 5:21).

4. It Shows the Uniqueness of Christ

The Virgin Birth shows that no one else has ever come into the world the same way as Jesus. The unique and miraculous nature of Jesus carried on through His entire life. His birth was a miracle. His public ministry consisted of miracles.

5. The Bible Says So

The fifth reason to believe in the Virgin Birth is because the Bible says so. The doctrine of the Virgin Birth and the credibility of Christianity go hand-in-hand."

Matthew records the birth of Jesus in Chapter 2:1

Matthew 2:1 - *Now when Jesus was born, in Bethlehem of Judaea in the days of Herod the king, behold, there came wise men from the east to Jerusalem. Bethlehem was located about 5 miles south of Jerusalem.*

Matthew 2:2 - *Saying, Where is he that is born King of the Jews? For "we have seen his star in the east and are come to worship him."*

The conversation of these wise men regarding Jesus, was a result of hearing prophecies from many years before. One such mention can be found in the book of Numbers Chapter 24 in which Balaam, one of several prophets said to Balak:

Numbers 24:15 - *And he took up his parable, and said, Balaam the son of Beor hath said, and the man whose eyes are open hath said:*

Numbers 24:16 - *He hath said, which heard the words of God, and knew the knowledge of the most High, which saw the vision of the Almighty, falling into a trance, and having his eyes open:*

Numbers 24:17 - *I shall see him, but not now: I shall behold him, but not nigh: there shall come a Star out of Jacob, and a Sceptre shall rise out of Israel, and shall smite the corners of Moab, and destroy all the children of Sheth.*

Numbers 24:18 - *And Edom shall be a possession, Seir also shall be a possession for his enemies; and Israel shall do valiantly.*

Numbers 24:19 - *Out of Jacob shall come he that shall have dominion and shall destroy him that remaineth of the city.*

In verse 17, Balaam speaks prophetically of "seeing him." Him being the Messiah who he would see, not now, but later. Balaam's reference to the word *star* was used to represent a symbol of reigning power among all nations and is also often used to refer to the rise of a king or monarch. The descriptive term "scepter" according to the *Illustration Dictionary of the Bible,* states "the official staff of a ruler symbolizing his authority and power. Sometimes the symbolism of a scepter refers to the Messiah who will rule from Israel, from the tribe of Judah. In the New Testament, the book of Hebrews describes Christ as the Son who "rules with a scepter of righteousness."

While Luke chapter 2 gives limited information on the childhood of Jesus, that information is limited, up until age 12, not much is written. There appears to be nothing recorded in the Bible of the life of Jesus from the age of approximately 12 until he re-emerged at age 30.

Luke 2:40 - *And the child grew, and waxed strong in spirit, filled with wisdom: and the grace of God was upon him.*

Luke 2:41 - *Now his parents went to Jerusalem every year at the feast of the Passover.*

Luke 2:42 - *And when he was twelve years old, they went up to Jerusalem after the custom of the feast.*

Luke 2:43 - *And when they had fulfilled the days, as they returned, the child Jesus tarried behind in Jerusalem; and Joseph and his mother knew not of it.*

Luke 2:44 - *But they, supposing him to have been in the company, went a day's journey; and they sought him among their kinsfolk Luke and acquaintance.*

Luke 2:45 - *And when they found him not, they turned back again to Jerusalem, seeking him.*

Luke 2:46 - *And it came to pass, that after three days they found him in the temple, sitting in the midst of the doctors, both hearing them, and asking them questions.*

Luke 2:47 - *And all that heard him were astonished at his understanding and answers.*

Luke 2:48 - *And when they saw him, they were amazed and his other said unto him, Son why hast thou thus dealt with us? behold, thy father and I have sought thee sorrowing.*

Luke 2:49 - *And he said unto them, How is it that ye sought me? Wist ye not that I must be about my Father's business?*

Luke 2:50 - *And they understood not the saying which he spake unto them.*

Luke 2:51 - *And he went down with them, and came to Nazareth, and was subject unto them: but his mother kept all these sayings in her heart.*

THE EIGHTEEN SILENT YEARS OF JESUS

Luke 2:52 - *And Jesus increased in wisdom and stature, and in favour with God and man.*

Verse 52 reflects on what seemed to be a period of absence of Jesus but was in essence, a time when the "silent or 18 years" was of significant importance. His life was undergoing a period of transformation to include his physical, moral, and spiritual stature.

In a brief synopsis of *The Eighteen Silent Years*[11] John Brown, M.A., sums it up in three parts—submission, work and growth.

Submission: The characteristic virtue of childhood, its natural and necessary condition. The daily round of home life, with its routine of duties, its continual calls for submission, often all the more difficult to obey because we cannot, even to ourselves, dignify them with the name of hardships or great trials – this Christ has consecrated by these eighteen silent years.

Work: Doing each day's work in its appointed time – be the work what it may—fitted Him for the future, when the work was different. Surely the lesson is not what you do, but how you do it.

Growth: (1) This does not necessarily mean imperfection. The child is not to blame because he is not a man all at once. It is the law of his being to grow. He lives by growth. Up to his measure he may be perfectly developed; but that measure, that capacity, is continually expanding. So, we learn to think of growth as inseparable from healthy human life, of progress as the law of our nature, of increase in wisdom as perfectly compatible with all moral and spiritual excellence. In Christ this earth has for once been permitted to witness

11 John Brown, M.A.

the natural development of a sinless childhood – development, not by sudden miracle, but by Divine indwelling. The glory that dwelt in Jesus shone in those eighteen quiet years in the orderly progress, step by step, of the boy to the youth, the youth to the man.

(2) For nothing can be plainer than this, that the Lord's humanity was real indeed. Every line of the gospel tells us this; every word of these verses, which record while they do not reveal, these eighteen years. We do not doubt it, indeed; perhaps we dwell on it with appreciation and thankfulness. But let us never forget that the same Lord, who thus lived and toiled, rose, ascended, lives, reigns. It is not simply by contemplation, even devout contemplation, of the perfectly human Jesus, that our spirits live. It is by personal fellowship with the God-man, as human now as ever, but God then in the days of His flesh, as now. This is the message of redemption, God's message to the Church and to the world, to the soul that suffers, sins, dies, to the word that sickens, staggers, swoons-God made man for you!"

Verse 52 is profound in just a few words; it gives us insight into the mystery of how Jesus matured and strengthened during this process. This verse states that Jesus "increased" in wisdom and stature, and in favour with God and man. While keeping His divine nature, he limited Himself to the attributes and powers as He walked in the flesh. He showed He was able to overcome sin and through the power of the Holy Spirit defeated Satan. His demonstration of walking as a sinless human was possible when we allow the baptism of the Spirit to transform our natural ability into supernatural attributes and power.

WHY CHRIST GAVE HIS LIFE FOR MANKIND

1. For the sins of man (see Galatians 1:4; Matthew 1:21, 26:28; 1 Corinthians15:3; 1 Peter 2:24)
2. That through Him, we might be delivered from the evil of this world (Galatians 1:4; Titus 2:14)

3. That through the Word, He might sanctify the church (Ephesians 5:25-26)
4. He became a ransom for all mankind (1 Timothy 2:6)
5. That through Him, all might be redeemed from all sin and iniquity

Paul, who persecuted Christians, was later converted and became the apostle to the Gentiles. He became a preacher and provided one of the clearest understandings of Christianity. Romans 15:29 give us an insight into how powerful Paul was as a teacher, preacher and writer of the gospels. Verse 29 – In his letter to the Romans, Paul goes on to state *"And I am sure that, when I come unto you, I shall come in the fullness of the blessing of the gospel of Christ."* This was Paul's way of stating his confidence in the truths and power of the gospel. He was so sure of its ability to inform and transform, that he told the Romans in his letters, that he would be coming with all the power and authority given to him by Christ Jesus. Paul possessed ALL the gifts and fruit of the Spirit through Christ Jesus. Paul was a powerful witness to the Word and the Works of Jesus Christ. Paul demonstrated a fervency to get that knowledge to all who would listen. He did not want to fall short of what God had assigned his hands to do.

Matthew 28:18 - *And Jesus came and spake unto them, saying: all power is given unto me in heaven and in earth.*

Matthew 28:19 - *Go ye therefore and teach all nations baptizing them in the name of the Father, and of the Son, and of the Holy Ghost.*

Matthew 28:20 - *Teaching them to observe all things whatsoever I have commanded you and lo, I am with you always, even unto the end of the world. Amen.*

Matthew 28:18-20 are some of the most important scriptures for the body of Christ to know, because it is here that God the Father gave all power to God the Son who was limited after He became "man." After the redemption of Jesus Christ, he again joined His Father and the Holy Spirit. The commandment gives all Christians the power and authority to carry on with the words that Jesus started while here on earth.

> **John 12:49** - *For I have not spoken of myself, but the Father which sent me, he gave me a commandment, what I should say, and what I should speak.*

In this scripture, as Jesus speaks, acknowledges that He speaks for the Father and speaks what the Father gives him to say.

CHAPTER 5

GOD THE HOLY SPIRIT

THE HOLY SPIRIT HAS THE DIRECT POWER OF OPERATIONS

The Holy Spirit is the third person of the Trinity, sent by both the Father and the Son. It is by the Holy Spirit, the works of Christ is carried out through the believer. The offices of the Spirit, also called the Comforter, are defined in detail later in this text. Having the direct power of operations, the Holy Spirit performs divine functions such as judging, pouring out the love of God, giving joy, hope, peace and faith. Dr. David Jeremiah refers to the Holy Spirit as being a "Divine Resident"12 whose presence changes us in seven ways:

1. We are born of the Spirit: This is a reference to the new birth that we experience when we accept Jesus Christ; and through faith now believe we will see the kingdom of God. (John 3:3)
2. We are indwelt by the Spirit: As a Christian, the Spirit dwells in us and helps us understand the things of God. (Romans 8:9)

3. We are baptized by the Spirit: As a member of the Body of Christ, we operate in conjunction with other Christians who are also part of the body. (1 Corinthian 12:13)
4. We are filled by the Spirit: Being filled with the Spirit requires we walk in a new light and must not grieve the Spirit by walking in any way that is disorderly. (Ephesians 5:18)
5. We are illuminated by the Spirit: Things that previously perplexed us, we are now enlightened and able to discern spiritual truths. (1 Corinthians 2:13)
6. We walk in the Spirit: As we live, we shall also walk in the Spirit by living a life of obedience to Jesus Christ. (Galatians 5:25)
7. We exhibit the Spirit: This is the true evidence of our transformation as our daily walk demonstrates love, joy, peace, longsuffering, kindness, goodness, faithfulness, gentleness and self-control that is fruit of the Spirit. (Galatians 5:22-23)

The Spirit desires to be the only resident in you. This indwelling of the Spirit is the assurance we have that we are equipped and able to resist the temptations of the world.

God, the Holy Spirit, was mentioned in several scriptures throughout the Bible. He gives strength for extraordinary situations as demonstrated in Judges 3. Here the Spirit of the Lord gave victory to Othniel, the first judge over Babylon, and added 40 years of peace.

Judges 3:9 - *And when the children of Israel cried unto the LORD, the LORD raised up a deliverer to the children of Israel, who delivered them, even Othniel the son of Kenaz, Caleb's younger brother.*

Judges 3:10 - *And the Spirit of the LORD came upon him, and he judged Israel, and went out to war: and the LORD delivered Chushan-rishathaim king of Mesopotamia into his hand; and his hand prevailed against Chushan-rishathaim.*

Judges 3:11 - *And the land had rest forty years. And Othniel the son of Kenaz died.*

The strength and power of the Holy Spirit is manifest through the scripture John 6:63-65.

John 6:63 - *It is the spirit that quickened; the flesh profiteth nothing: the words that I speak unto you, they are spirit and they are life.*

John 6:64 - *But there are some of you that believe not. For Jesus know from the beginning who they were that believed not, and who should betray him.*

John 6:65 - *And he said, Therefore said I unto you, that no man can come unto me except it were given unto him of my Father.*

Verse 63 explains that only He (God the Holy Spirit) can give you a change of heart. Only the spirit is able to make the spirit of man come alive, to become stimulated enough to want to make a change in our everyday life. This scripture denotes the strength and power of the Holy Spirit. Verse 64 declares that Jesus knew from the beginning those who would believe and those who would betray or believe Him not. So, as the Holy Spirit pricks our hearts and our spirit, it causes us to want to make a change for the better. To put aside the fleshly things that are not profitable.

Matthew 3:16 - *And Jesus when he was baptized, went up straightway out of the water: and lo, the heavens were opened unto him and he saw the Spirit of God descending like a dove and lightning upon him:*

Matthew 3:17 - *And lo a voice from heaven, saying, This is my beloved Son, in whom I am well pleased.*

Matthew 3:16-17 references all three persons of the Trinity. Jesus sees the Spirit of God when He came up out of the water; and God the Father claims Jesus as His own son.

Charles Stanley also states "The way of redemption showcases these roles in a clear manner. The Father designed and organized how mankind would be redeemed (Galatians 4:4-5). He set into motion a complex set of events, actions, and prophecies which culminated in the life and death of a Savior. The Son carried out the plan (John 6:37-38). He followed the Father's instructions to come to earth, even though that meant He would have to die. The Holy Spirit sees to it that every person feels a call toward God's saving grace (John 14:26, John 16:8; Romans1:19-20). Furthermore, He transforms the lives and hearts of those who receive salvation through Jesus Christ.

The Father, Son and Spirit are equal in their divine attributes. Yet each relates to mankind in a different way because each one has a specific role. It's very important to understand this distinction. We do not have three Gods; we have one God, in three persons, functioning uniquely and perfectly."[12]

Luke 24:45 again gives us insight into the power of the Holy Spirit.

Then opened he their understanding that they might understand the scripture.

---

12 Charles Stanley

This scripture gives an explanation of how He literally opens up our understanding of the Bible (God's word). The purpose here of course, is that we might have a clear understanding of what we can expect from the Word of God.

Acts 1:2-3 also gives insight into God the Holy Spirit.

> *Acts 1:2 - Until the day in which he was taken up after that he through the Holy Ghost had given commandments unto the apostles whom he had chosen:*

> *Acts 1:3 - To whom also he showed himself alive after his passion by many infallible proofs being seen of them forty days and speaking of the things pertaining to the kingdom of God.*

Here, the scripture shows us that after Jesus ascended to heaven, the works that he did are now continued through the Holy Spirit. The Holy Spirit now performs as an executive of God to continue the works of Jesus.

In John 3:6, we get another look into who the Holy Spirit is.

> *Jesus answered and said, unto him, Verily, verily, I say unto thee, Except a man be born again, he cannot see the kingdom God.*

I really like this scripture because there is so much here to exegesis before we can get to the full meaning. Dakes Notes and highlights, on page 212, the context of the word "except" which gives us the requirements for how we can "see" the kingdom of God as follows:

1. *Except ye repent ye shall all likewise perish (Luke 13:1-5)*
2. *Except ye become converted and become as little children ye shall not enter the kingdom of heaven (Matthew 18:3)*

3. *Except a man be born again, he cannot see the kingdom of God (John 3:3; 1John 2:29)*
4. *Except a man be born of water anode the Spirit, he cannot enter the kingdom of God (John. 3:5)*
5. *Except ye eat the flesh of the Son of man, and drink His blood, ye have no life in you (John. 6:53)*
6. *Except your righteousness shall exceed the righteousness of the scribes and Pharisees, ye shall in no case enter into the kingdom of heaven (Matthew 5:20)*
7. *Except ye abide in me . . . he is cast for as a branch, and is withered, and men gather them and cast them into the fire, and they are burned (John. 15:4-6)*

Dakes also references the words "he cannot see" the kingdom of God. Here, the intent of the Holy Spirit is not to cause you to see with the natural eye, but to use your spiritual senses to actually become more aware of what the kingdom of God can bring to us. It gives us a glimpse into the benefits of what God has to offer us when we follow His instructions. It is here that we find, the Word is not referring to an actual new birth which is impossible, but rather a spiritual birth or baptism into the Holy Spirit.

In John 14:26 we are able to see how He helped His disciples remember Jesus Christ. Through the Holy Spirit we are also the benefactor of this gift.

> *But the Comforter, which is the Holy Ghost, whom the Father will send in my name, he shall teach you all things and bring all things to your remembrance, whatsoever I have said unto you.*

Dakes (page 196) refers to the "Comforter" as the one "called to the side of another for help or counsel. The Spirit is our "paraclete or helper" on earth and Christ is the "paraclete or helper" in Heaven.

John 16:8 - *And when he is come, he will reprove the word of sin, and of righteousness, and of judgment.*

CHARACTERISTICS OF THE SPIRIT

Dakes explanation (page 212) gives us a look at twelve offices of the Spirit:

1. Begetter of the new birth:

In John 3:3 we see that the Holy Spirit was the generator of the knowledge wherein Jesus said, Verily, verily, I say unto thee, Except a man be born again, he cannot see the kingdom of God. In vs 4, Nicodemus initially takes the meaning of "born again" as the natural birth as if a mother delivers a child. Knowing that as an adult, old man, that was an impossibility. However, this new birth required a God inspired transformation of oneself to practice what is righteous and holy. Then again in vs 5, Jesus spake, Except a man be born of water and of the Spirit, he cannot enter into the kingdom of God. The word "water" here means being born by the Word of God, the acceptance of salvation of accepting Jesus Chris as our Lord and Savior.

2. Life-giver:

Romans 8:11 gives a great explanation of the Holy Spirit giving life. It states "But if the Spirit of him that raised Jesus from the dead dwell in you, he that raised up Christ from the dead shall also quicken your mortal bodies by His Spirit that dwelleth in you. Hence, it is the Holy Spirit that makes the spirit come alive.

3. Imparter of power:

The Words Jesus spoke in Acts 1:8 offers one of the most powerful representations of how magnificent God is. How in His infinite wisdom gives to us through the person of the Holy Spirit one of the most powerful tools we can have as a Christian.

> *"But ye shall receive power, after that the Holy Ghost is come upon you and ye shall be witnesses unto me both in Jerusalem and to all Judaea, and in Samaria, and unto the uttermost part of the earth."*

Praise be unto God for me being one of many who dwell in one of the uttermost parts of the earth. The uttermost represents those areas where the Great Commission is to take place. Where those who were chosen and accepted the mission of going into all nations to teach and baptize them in the name of the Father and of the Son, and of the Holy Spirit. The Spirit will empower them to not only meet this commitment, but to prosper exceedingly well in that assignment.

4. Eternal Comforter or Helper:

John 14:26 states in the Words of Jesus,

> *But the Comforter, which is the Holy Ghost, whom the Father will send in my name, he shall teach you all things, and bring all things to your remembrance, whatsoever I have said unto you.*

5. Teacher of Truth:

John 14:17 - *Even the Spirit of truth; who the world cannot receive, because it seeth him not neither knoweth him: but ye know him; for he dwelleth with you, and shall be in you.*

Because the Holy Spirit is the Spirit of God, there is only truth in Him. He cannot lie. He will only lead, guide, encourage, strengthen, and empower. He causes the natural man to be transformed by way of a quickening within the spirit, which in turn, creates a supernatural being that is able to respond over and above that which you normally would, and in a manner than is undeniably supernatural. Those who are unsaved are not able to have this supernatural experience because they do not believe.

6. Reminder of all truth:

In addition to John 14:26, as previously stated above, The Holy Spirit comes to bring us many truths that some may not be ready or willing to accept. He comes to expose and convict those in need of correction; and to bring justice to those who live righteously.

7. Guide into all truth:

In John 16:13 Jesus says

> *"Howbeit when the Spirit of truth, is come, he will guide you into all truth: for he shall not speak of himself; but whatsoever he shall hear, that shall he speak: and he will shew you things to come.*

Verse 13 comes with promise. A prophetic word that will come to pass.

8. Revealer of Christ:

In addition to the scripture in verses 13 above and 14 reads:

> **John 16:14** - *He shall glorify me: for he shall receive of mine and shall shew it unto you.*

> **John 16:15** - *All things the Father hath are mine: therefore, said I, that he shall take of mine, and shall shew it unto you.*

God the Father through his Son Jesus Christ reveals in part, when the Holy Spirit would come and what He would do for us.

9. Revealer of events

John 16:13 holds a prophecy of future revelations in this scripture:

Howbeit when he, the Spirit of truth, is come, he will guide you into all truth; for he shall not speak of himself; but whatsoever he shall hear, that shall he speak; and he will shew you things to come.

10. Glorifier of Christ

John 16:14 - *He shall glorify me; for he shall receive of mine and shall shew it unto you.*

Here Jesus speaks of the Holy Spirit that would come after his ascension; and remain to continue to do the works through the believer who has received the Holy Spirit through baptism.

11. Chief Witness for Christ

In Acts 1:8, Jesus says we would be the chief witnesses for Christ,

But ye shall receive power, after that the Holy Ghost is come jupon you; and ye shall be witnesses unto me, both in Jerusalem, and in all Judaea, and in Samaria, and unto the uttermost part of the earth.

12. Convincer of sin, righteousness, and judgment

Acts 1:9 - *Of sin, because they believe not on me;*

Acts 1:10 - *Of righteousness, because I go to my Father, and ye see me no more;*

Acts 1:11 - *Of judgment, because the prince of this world is judged.*

In verses 9-11, Jesus again declares the works of the Holy Spirit throughout the world. He says because those that believe not, is the basis and source of sinfulness that will cause men to be damned. That man's hubris and establishing his own righteousness is in conflict with the righteousness of Christ. While the believers will avoid the judgment of damnation; those who chose to refuse to believe will be damned along with Satan.

To avoid that great calamity, the Holy Spirit remains to continue the works that Christ can no longer perform, because He is now with His Father.

WHY GOD SENT THE HOLY SPIRIT

Acts 1:4-5 tells us why God sent the Holy Spirit.

> **Acts 1:4** - *And being assembled together with them, commanded them that they should not depart from Jerusalem, but wait for the promise of the Father, which saith he, ye have heard of me.*

> **Acts 1:5** - *For John truly baptized with water, but ye shall be baptized with the Holy Ghost not many days hence.*

The following scriptures are proof that the Holy Spirit existed from the beginning, even before the crucifixion of Jesus, and as referenced in the Old Testament, and empowered those He touched. The Holy Spirit would often come upon men to encourage and strengthen them.

Moses and the 70 elders of Israel in Numbers 11:25-26 – And the LORD said unto Moses, Gather unto me seventy men of the elders of Israel, whom thou knowest to be the elders of the people, and officers over them, and bring them unto the tabernacle of the congregation, that they may stand there with thee. And I will come down and talk with thee there: and I will take of the spirit which *is* upon thee and will put it upon them; and they shall bear the burden of the people with thee, that thou bear it not thyself alone.

1 Samuel 10:6 reflects Saul's conversion as God spoke to him – And the Spirit of the LORD will come upon thee, and thou shalt prophesy with them, and shall be turned into another man. God gave him another heart as he was born again through faith, redeemed and made a new creature. Unfortunately, Saul backslid by choosing to break the commandments of God and Saul later met his demise by committing suicide.

In Samuel 16:13 when Saul took the horn of oil, and anointed David in the midst of his brethren and the Spirit of the LORD came upon David from that day forward.

WHAT IS THE FRUIT OF THE SPIRIT?

As our Comforter and Helper, the Spirit wants to ensure we have all the tools that will keep us in harmony with God's Word and God's will. One of the many goals and functions of the Spirit is to provide us with the strength needed to accomplish a fruitful and successful walk with Jesus Christ and gain the approval from God the Father.

Fruit in this context are not edible fruits or vegetables but shows the result or action from our deeds or hard work. The "fruit of our labor" implies we have something to show for our work other than a paycheck.

Paul lists the nine specific behaviors that should result from our work as Christians.

1. Love: According to Greek interpretations, this love is not a brotherly (philos) love, or sexual (eros) love, but a perfect (agape) love that only God can give. Agape love produces a desire to help others. Biblical love is a choice that expresses itself in loving ways, and always seeks the welfare of others.

Philippians 2:2 - *Fulfil ye my joy, that ye be likeminded, having the same love, being of one accord, of one mind.*

2. Joy: This type of joy celebrates God's favor and grace and expresses the happiness that is not the result of anything that we've done for ourselves.

James 1:2-3 - *My brethren, count it all joy when ye fall into divers temptations; Knowing this, that the trying of your faith worketh patience.*

3. Peace: With God, the spirit of peace is possible no matter what our circumstances may be. With God, we are able to experience peace, safety and security. With God's peace we don't fear the instability of the circumstances which life often brings.

Romans 8:6 - *For to be carnally minded is death; but to be spiritually minded is life and peace.*

4. Longsuffering: The Spirit empowers us to endure the challenges, provocations, offenses and injuries we encounter on a daily basis without resentment or murmuring. We are able to demonstrate our ability to persevere.

1 Timothy 1:16 - *Howbeit for this cause I obtained mercy, that in me first Jesus Christ might shew forth all longsuffering, for a pattern to them which should hereafter believe on him to life everlasting.*

5. Gentleness: One who has a disposition of being soft-spoken, not boisterous, even-tempered, and presents themselves as being gracious in mannerisms.

2 Timothy 2:25 - *In meekness instructing those that oppose themselves, if God peradventure will give them repentance to the acknowledging of the truth.*

6. Kindness: This characteristic also implies gentleness or someone who behaves properly, has moral integrity without getting caught in self-righteousness or judgment. One who is virtuous and generous, and God-like in life and conduct.

Ephesians 2:7 - *That in the ages to come he might shew the exceeding riches of his grace in his kindness toward us through Christ Jesus.*

7. Faith: A character trait that combines dependability and trust based on our confidence in God and His eternal faithfulness. It is our belief in God and our certainty that Jesus is the Messiah whom we obtain eternal salvation.

2 Thessalonians 1:11 - *Wherefore also we pray always for you, that our God would count you worthy of this calling, and fulfil all the good pleasure of his goodness, and the work of faith with power.*

8. Meekness: Characterizes one who has been placed in a position of weakness, but able to show strength by maintaining control.

Galatians 6:1 - *Brethren, if a man be overtaken in a fault, ye which are spiritual, restore such an one in the spirit of meekness; considering thyself, lest thou also be tempted.*

Temperance: One who is able to exercise self-control of the flesh. To say no to flesh gives us the power to say yes to the Spirit.

Galatians 5:16 - *This I say then, Walk in the Spirit, and ye shall not fulfil the lust of the flesh.*

God and Jesus Christ sent the Spirit to lead and empower all Christians. The fruit of the Spirit is produced by the Spirit to enable us to manifest all of the characteristics of Christ as we grow. The Spirit knows we need time to grow and mature as edible fruit does but is there to strengthen us as we fight against the obstacles we encounter from day to day. As we submit ourselves to the Spirit of God, His goal remains to shape and mold us into the image of Christ.

WHAT ARE THE GIFTS OF THE SPIRIT?

The Spirit continues to perform as an executive of God to continue the work of Jesus Christ. That work includes seeing that we enjoy the benefits of what God has to offer us when we follow His instructions. According to 1 Corinthians 12:7-11 shows further proof our Comforter and Helper wants to provide us with every opportunity to educate us. Another function or role of the Spirit is to distribute the "Nine Gifts of the Holy Spirit". These are supernatural gifts according to scripture and available to all Christians. The nine gifts fall into three classifications: The Gifts of Revelations or "mind gifts;" The Gifts of Inspiration or "vocal gifts;" and The Gifts of Power or "working gifts."

1 Corinthians 12:1 - *Now concerning spiritual gifts, brethren, I would not have you ignorant*

1 Corinthians 12:7 - *But the manifestation of the Spirit is given to every man to profit withal.*

1 Corinthians 12:8 - *For to one is given by the Spirit the word of wisdom; to another the word of knowledge by the same Spirit;*

1 Corinthians 12:9 - *To another faith by the same Spirit; to another the gifts of healing by the same Spirit;*

1 Corinthians 12:10 - *To another the working of miracles; to another prophecy; to another discerning of spirits; to another divers kinds of tongues; to another the interpretation of tongues.*

1. Gifts of Revelation or "Mind Gifts"
    a. The Word of Wisdom – A supernatural revelation or insight into God's divine will and purpose, revealing how to solve a problem.
    b. The Word of Knowledge – A supernatural revelation or insight into God's divine will or plan to know things that could not be known of oneself.
    c. Discerning of Spirits – The supernatural revelation or insight into the realm of spirits, to detect them and their plan and includes reading the minds of men.
2. Gifts of Inspiration or "Vocal Gifts"
3. Prophecy - The supernatural utterance in the native tongue. It is a miracle of divine utterance, not conceived

by human thought or reasoning. It includes speaking unto men to edification, exhortation, and comfort.

   a. Divers Kinds of Tongues – The supernatural utterance in other languages that are not known to the speaker.
   b. The Interpretation of Tongues – The supernatural ability to interpret in the native tongue what is uttered in other languages not known by the one who interprets by the Spirit.

4. Gifts of Power or "Working Gifts"
   a. Gift of Faith – The supernatural ability to believe God without human doubt, unbelief, and reasoning.
   b. The Gift of Healing – The healing of all manner of sickness by supernatural power, without human aid or medicine.
   c. The Working of Miracles – The supernatural power to intervene in the ordinary course of nature, and to counteract natural laws if necessary.

CHAPTER 6

HOW THE TRINITY WORK IN CONCERT

THE TRINITY VS OTHERS WHO WORK IN CONCERT WITH EVERYDAY LIFE

Here is a brief and perhaps more easily understood analogy of looking at the Trinity. A different perspective may provide more clarity into the connection between the interworking of the Trinity. We can somewhat bridge the gap when we see how the interworkings of other organizations all come together to perform in concert with one another. Often it takes seeing those things that are visible, before we can accept imagining those things that are invisible.

To put things into perspective, here are a few examples of organizations that work in concert with one another. But just before that, let's look at a scripture that speaks to how all things in life work together.

> **Ephesians 4:11** - *And he gave some apostles, and some prophets, and some evangelist, and some pastors, and teachers;*

> **Ephesians 4:12** - *For the perfecting of the saints, for the work of the ministry, for the edifying of the body of Christ:*

Ephesians 4:13 - *Till we all come in the unity of the faith, and of the knowledge of the Son of God, unto a perfect man perfect man, unto the measure of the stature of the fulness of Christ:*

Ephesians 4:14 - *That we henceforth be no more children, tossed to and fro, and carried about with every wind of doctrine, by the sleight of men, and cunning craftiness, whereby they lie in wait to deceive;*

Ephesians 4:15 - *But speaking the truth in love, may grow up into him in all things, which is the head, even Christ:*

Ephesians 4:16 - *From whom the whole body fitly joined together and compacted by that which every joint supplieth, accordingly to the effectual working in the measure of every part, maketh increase of the body unto the edifying of itself in love.*

The essence here is that God wants everything to work in unison and in conjunction with His intended purpose.

Example 1: One analogy is to look at a finely tuned orchestra. To shorten the process, I'll only point out the main parts. Consider the song or music writer, the conductor, and those that play the instruments. Only the songwriter knows how the finished product should sound before it can be delivered to the human ear. That sound should be set to not only appeal to the human ear, but to maximize the effects on the human heart. Music is meant to stir the heart of the hearer. Music is an experience. The conductor must then be artful and skillful enough to be able to translate the intention of the writer of the music to the orchestra. That person must be able to convey to each instrumentalist the importance of how much, how little to manage their part in this effort. Then finally, no one and no instrument should make an effort to "drown out" the intent or purpose of the others but be "fitly joined together" to present a masterpiece through music.

Example 2: Take a look at automobile manufacturing. Several workers with specific skill sets are assigned to work at a factory that is designed to make a certain part, that is then shipped or delivered to a different location before all the parts/pieces can be assembled to become a complete unit. Several designers, supervision, cost estimators, quality control inspectors, and many others all work in concert to make the "initial designers'" dream or idea come to fruition. One automobile, many parts, many participants in the building and perfecting of that machine.

Example 3: We know without a doubt that the medical profession represents doctors who are some of the most gifted and knowledgeable professionals. But even with their gifts and talent, they cannot succeed without the assistance of a medical community of people who are also gifted. That includes those with specific skill sets to meet the needs of all the various sicknesses or diseases that mankind may encounter. Such as nurses, x-ray technicians, phlebotomist, radiologist and many others. Specialists in all areas of the medical profession are part of the effort to be "fitly join together" to work in concert for the good of their patient. Some may agree with how the medical community works, according to scripture, everything that is made was made by God. God made the man that made the medicine. God distributes the specific gifts and talents we each have. God made everything that goes into the making of medicines, equipment and machinery necessary to diagnose and treat sicknesses. That does not negate the fact that God gave us the power and authority to lay hands on the sick that they might be healed in the name of Jesus.

The three examples above provide a different perspective on how more than one person or persons can work together to provide or convey a specific thought or idea, or work toward one specific goal. So then, it is no small wonder that

God in all His magnificence, authority and wonder, can in fact present to us a spiritual belief system that works the same way all His other creations work.

With these explanations, hopefully it's easier for you to understand how there can be three distinct parts or persons that work together for the greater good of mankind. If man can maneuver through the complexities of manufacturing, making music and the medical industries, surely, he is able to comprehend the mysteries God has laid out before us. These mysteries are made known to only those who love God enough to trust in all of His word written specifically to guide us as we travel through the roadblocks of life.

There are no earthly examples that can fully explain the mystery of the Trinity. But there are many unscriptural examples of things that can illustrate the Trinity although each has some flaw or inconsistency:

- The three-part nature of man (body, soul and spirit). Man possesses a body, a soul, and a spirit. But at death the body is buried; the spirit goes to be with the Lord. You cannot separate the Trinity.
- A three-leaf clover has the same stem but can be separated one from the other. The Trinity cannot be separated.
- A tree has roots, a trunk, and branches. But some or all of their parts can be separated.
- Fire has three things to exist: fuel, heat and oxygen. If one is removed the fire goes out.

THINGS WE BELIEVE BUT CANNOT SEE

The purpose of this section is to point out the comparison of those things we believe because we can see them versus those things we believe and cannot see. It can be perplexing to admit there are things we cannot see, but know they exist.

Wind - Air - Oxygen - Gravity - Sound - Heat - Cold
Emotions - Life - Smell - Taste - Thoughts - Imagination
Energy - Electricity

GOD'S CARES FOR ALL OF HIS CREATION

The beauty of the heavenly skies is best described in Psalms 19:1.

> *The heavens declare the glory of God; and the firmament sheweth his handywork.*

We all can see the beauty in the earth and sky, and the many things we attribute to God's handywork. Things that have a significant impact on our daily existence.

Mountains/Dry Land:

> **Job 26:8** - *He bindeth up the waters in his thick clouds; and the cloud is not rent under them.*

Even though millions of tons of water are drawn up from the ocean into the clouds, the clouds don't break and let their water out all at once. Here we find that God creates a sprinkler system to water the dry lands as He sees fit.

> **Matthew 6:26** - *Behold the fowl of the air: for they sow not, neither do they reap, nor gather into barns, yet your heavenly Father feedeth them. Are ye not much better than they?*

This is God's way of caring for us. God's providence is over all creation, not only birds and plants that never buy, sell, manufacturer, or labor. God would not have any one to perish. Through the works of the Trinity, God the Father has created a plan and made it plain. God the Son, Jesus Christ our Lord and Savior has implemented the plan of redemption by His sacrifice on the cross. The Holy Spirit administers the plan as He strengthens us to walk into all righteousness.

Ephesians 4:3 - *Endeavoring to keep the unity of the Spirit in the bond of peace,*

Ephesians 4:4 - *There is one body, and one Spirit, even as ye are called in one hope of your calling;*

Ephesians 4:5 - *One Lord, one faith, one baptism*

Ephesians 4:6 - *One God and Father of all, who is above all, and through all, and in you all.*

Ephesians 4:3-6 - speaks to the sevenfold unity of God and man in that there is but:

1. ***One body*** that is the church,
2. ***One Spirit*** that is the Holy Spirit,
3. ***One hope***, that is the call to all Christians,
4. ***One Lord*** that the Our Lord and savior Jesus Christ,
5. ***One faith*** that is the teaching of the gospel which is the doctrine of Jesus Christ,
6. ***One baptism***, that is being baptized into the body of Christ,
7. ***One God***, that is the Father of all.

Romans 1:19 - *Because that which may be known of God is manifest in them; for God hath shewed it unto them.*

Romans 1:20 - *For the invisible things of him from the creation of the world are clearly seen, being understood by the things that are made, even his eternal power and Godhead; so that they are without excuse.*

This scripture lays out some of the most powerful evidence of the Trinity. Although we cannot see the all-powerful, all-knowing, all-eternal God, we cannot disregard the created things we can see with our own eyes. God has allowed us to experience His creation. God further reveals to us, through the Holy Spirit, the magnificence of His creation.

SUMMARY

As mentioned earlier, there are several reasons why I put pen to paper in writing this book. The most significant challenge was to acknowledge the commandment of Jesus in Matthew 28:19-20.

This challenge was also to present this book in a manner where the truths of the Bible could be easily understood. To reach and teach those who would be open to receiving the Gospel of Jesus Christ and follow through with the commands He has given. I felt it was extremely important that people be exposed to a book that offers a simpler way to understand how the Trinity can and will work in their lives. How they can pursue the promise of "eternal life" and not perish. The path to this abundant life will be made plain when they are enlightened with these truths.

Having the gifts of a teacher and an evangelist, I've always yearned to reach and teach the people of God. So, as I continue to minister through this project, my prayer is that this book would find itself in places I may have in times past desired to go, but up to now have not. I pray also that the miles I have yet to travel might be preceded by the written word through this book. As the reader completes this book, I'm confident the Spirit of God will lead them to have a closer relationship with God as their knowledge increases, so shall their relationship with Him.

And for those who have not accepted Jesus Christ as their Lord and Savior, they would do so as the word of God ministers to them. That they would pray the "sinners' prayer" of salvation

"Lord, I'm a sinner. Come into my heart, forgive me for those things I have said, done and thought that have not been pleasing in thy sight. Forgive me and accept me this day as I ask this prayer in Jesus' name." Amen

I seek to provide both old and new believers with a simple, truthful, and hopefully, more definitive walk through scripture while trying to attain the goal of getting a better understanding of the offices, functions and existence of the Holy Trinity. This book gives a presentation that will layout terms which show how all the parts of the Holy Trinity is connected in a way that will personally enlighten each reader. Because the focus is on getting to know each person of the Holy Trinity, this book is purposely guided by scripture so the reader can see, understand and correctly interpret how all three persons of the Trinity are working on their behalf on a daily basis.

It's also important to know the context in which the name of each person of the Trinity was used in scripture. This new knowledge will give the reader the insight into just how omniscient, omnipotent and omnipresent God is. For God wants none to perish but come into the full knowledge of the truth. That is not to say some will not perish, but God's plan allows for all who desire a life of abundance, would decide to choose His will.

My recommendations are to read, study, and research the Bible on the Holy Trinity. In doing so, one should consider the list of Scripture references to the Trinity overall, as well as God the Father, God the Son and God the Holy Spirit from the list on the pages that follow.

BOOKS OF THE BIBLE: COMPLETE LIST WITH AUTHORS AND APPROXIMATE TIME WRITTEN*

OLD TESTAMENT

Pentateuch:

- Genesis, written by Moses (1688 B.C.)
- Exodus, written by Moses (1688 B.C.)
- Leviticus, written by Moses (1686 B.C.)
- Numbers, written by Moses (1440-1400 B.C.)
- Deuteronomy, written by Moses (1200 B.C.)

*Times written are approximate

The Books of History:

Joshua written by Joshua (except the part relating to his death) (1646-1616 B.C.)
Judges written by Samuel, Nathan, Gad (1126 B.C.)
Ruth written by Samuel, Nathan, Gad (1163-1123 B.C.)
1 Samuel written by Samuel, Nathan, Gad (1204-1035 B.C.)
2 Samuel, written by Samuel, Nathan, Gad (743-683 B.C.)
1 Kings & 2 Kings written by Jeremiah (1046-616 B.C.)
1 Chronicles & 2 Chronicles written by Isaiah and Ezekiel (1279-461B.C.)
Ezekiel written by Ezekiel (546-461 B.C.)
Nehemiah written by Nehemiah or Ezekiel or perhaps both (446-430 B.C.)
Esther written by Ezekiel (516-506 B.C.)

The Books of Poetry and Writings:

Job (uncertain but writer could be Job and Moses (about 430 B.C.)
Psalms written in five (5) parts, authors Moses, David, Solomon and others (1500-450 B.C.)

- Book 1 includes Psalms 1-41 called the Genesis book
- Book 2 includes Psalms 42-72 called the Exodus book
- Book 3 includes Psalms 73-89 called the Leviticus book
- Book 4 includes Psalms 90-106 called the Numbers book
- Book 5 includes 107-160 called the Deuteronomy book

Proverbs written mostly by Solomon (about 1,000 B.C.)
Ecclesiastes written by Solomon (1,000 B.C.)
Song of Solomon written by Solomon (1,000 B.C.)

<u>Major Prophets:</u>

Isaiah written by Isaiah (792-722 B.C.)

Jeremiah written by Jeremiah (685-616 B.C.)

Lamentations written by Jeremiah (616 B.C.)

Ezekiel written by Ezekiel (622-600 B.C.)

Daniel written by Daniel (616-536 B.C.)

<u>Minor Prophets:</u>

Hosea written by Hosea (781-711 B.C.)

Joel written by Joel (795-755 B.C.)

Amos written by Amos (824-810 B.C.)

Obadiah written by Obadiah (899-795 B.C.)

Jonah written by Jonah (783-824 B.C.)

Micah written by Micah (772-722 B.C.)

Nahum written by Nahum (786-757 B.C.)

Habakkuk written by Habakkuk (680-648 B.C.)

Zephaniah written by Zephaniah (679-648 B.C.)

Haggai written by Haggai (557-525 B.C.)

Zechariah written by Zechariah (500 B.C.)

Malachi written by Malachi (557-525 B.C.)

NEW TESTAMENT

<u>Gospels:</u>

Matthew written by Matthew (A.D. 35-55)

Mark written by John Mark (A.D. 57-63)

Luke written by Luke (A.D. 60)

John written by John the disciple (A.D. 90)

<u>History:</u>

Acts written by Luke (A.D. 65)

Pauline Epistles:

Romans written by Paul (A.D.55-60)

1 Corinthians & 2 Corinthians written by Paul (A.D. 60)

Galatians written by Paul (A.D. 60)

Ephesians written by Paul (A.D. 60)

Philippians written by Paul (A.D. 60)

Colossians written by Paul (A.D. 60)

1 Thessalonians & 2 Thessalonians written by Paul (A.D. 54-55)

1 Timothy & 2 Timothy written by Paul (A.D. 60)

Titus written by Paul (A.D. 60)

Philemon written by Paul (A.D. 50-70)

General Epistles:

Hebrews (A.D. 65-70) Some debate, but likely Paul

James written by James the half-brother of Jesus Christ (A.D. 45)

1 Peter & 2 Peter written by Peter (About A.D. 60)

1 John, 2 John & 3 John written by John the Apostle (About A.D. 90)

Jude written by Jude (A.D. 60)

Prophecy:

Revelation written by John (A.D. 90)

BIBLE VERSES THAT REFERENCE ALL THREE MEMBERS OF THE TRINITY

OLD TESTAMENT:

Genesis 1:26

And God said, Let us make man in our image, after our likeness: and let them have dominion over the fish of the sea, and over the fowl of the air, and over the cattle, and over all the earth, and over every creeping thing that creepeth upon the earth.

Genesis 3:22

And the Lord God said, Behold, the man is become as one of us, to know good and evil: and now, lest he put forth his hand, and take also of the tree of life, and eat, and live forever.

Genesis 11:7

Go to, let us go down, and there confound their language, that they may not understand one another's speech.

Isaiah 6:8

Also I heard the voice of the Lord, saying, Whom shall I send, and who will go for us? Then said I, Here am I; send me.

Isaiah 48:16

Come ye near unto me, hear ye this; I have not spoken in secret from the beginning; from time that it was, there am I: and now the Lord God, and his Spirit, hath sent me.

Psalms 51:11-13

11 - *Cast me not away from thy presence, and take not thy holy spirit from me.*

12 - *Restore unto me the joy of thy salvation; and uphold me with thy free spirit.*

13 - *Then will I teach transgressions thy ways; and sinners shall be converted unto thee.*

Psalms 110:1

The LORD said unto my Lord, Sit thou at my right hand, until I make thine enemies thy footstool.

NEW TESTAMENT:

Matthew 3:16

And Jesus, when he was baptized, went up straightway out of the water: and lo, the heavens were opened unto him, and he saw the Spirit of God descending like a dove, and lighting upon him.

Matthew 28:19

Go ye therefore, and teach all nations, baptizing them in the name of the Father, and of the Son, and of the Holy Ghost:

Luke 3:22

And the Holy Ghost descended in a bodily shape like a dove upon him, and a voice came from heaven, which said Thou art my beloved Son; in thee I am well pleased.

John 14:26

But the Comforter, which is the Holy Ghost, whom the Father will send in my name, he shall teach you all things, and bring all things to your remembrance, whatsoever I have said unto you.

John 15:26

26 - *But when the Comforter is come, whom I will send unto you from the Father, seen the Spirit of truth, which proceedeth from the Father, he shall testify of me.*

27 - *And ye also shall bear witness, because ye have been with me from the beginning*

Acts 1:4

And, being assembled together with them, commanded them that they should not depart from Jerusalem, but wait for the promises of the Father, which saith he, ye have heard of me.

Acts 2:33

Therefore being by the right hand of God exalted, and having received of the Father the promise of the Holy Ghost, he hath shed forth this, which ye now see and hear.

Acts 10:38

How God anointed Jesus of Nazareth with the Holy Ghost and with power: who went about doing good and healing all that were oppressed of the devil; for God was with him.

Romans 8:9

Be ye are not in the flesh, but in the Spirit, if so be that the Spirit of God dwell in you. Now if any man have not the Spirit of Christ, he is none of his.

1 Corinthians 6:11

And such were some of you: but ye are washed, but ye are sanctified, but ye are justified in the name of the Lord Jesus, and by the Spirit of our God.

2 Corinthians 13:14

The grace of the Lord Jesus Christ, and the love of God, and the communion of the Holy Ghost, be with you all. Amen.

Galatians 4:6

And because ye are sons, God hath sent forth the Spirit of his Son into your hearts, crying, Abba, Father.

Ephesians 1:17

That the God of our Lord Jesus Christ; the Father of glory, may give unto you the spirit of wisdom and revelation in the knowledge of him.

Ephesians 2:18

For through him we both have access by one Spirit unto the Father.

Ephesians 2:22

In whom ye also are builded together for an habitation of God through the Spirit.

Hebrews 9:14

How much more, shall the blood of Christ, who through the eternal Spirit offered himself without spot to God, purge your conscience from dead works to serve the living God.

1 Peter 1:2

Elect according to the foreknowledge of God the Father, through sanctification of the Spirit, unto obedience and sprinkling of the blood of Jesus Christ: Grace unto you, and peace, be multiplied.

SCRIPTURE REFERENCE FOR NAMES AND MEANING OF EACH PERSON OF THE TRINITY

GOD THE FATHER

The Names of Elohim
Genesis 14:18 -20

El-Elyon: The Most High God
Meaning – indicates he possesses the heaven and earth; shows God as being the Mighty One and worthy to be praised.

Genesis 14:18 - *And Melchizedek king of Salem brought forth brad and wine and he was the priest of the most high God.*

Genesis 14:19 - *And he blessed him, and said, Blessed be Abram of the most high God, possessor of heaven and earth:*

Genesis 14:20 - *And blessed be the most high God, which hath delivered thine enemies into thy hand. And he gave him tithes of all.*

El-Shaddai: The Almighty God

Genesis 17:1-2

Meaning – The God who is able to give strength, supplies all your needs; the life-giver to Abraham and Sarah

Genesis 17:1 - *And when Abram was ninety years old and nine, the Lord appeared to Abram, and said unto him, I am the Almighty God; walk before me, and be thou perfect.*

Genesis 17:2 - *And I will make my covenant between me and thee and will multiply thee exceedingly.*

El-Olam: The Everlasting God

Genesis 21:33

Meaning – He is the Eternal one and the author of all eternal things, never ending, always, perpetual.

And Abraham planted a grove in Beersheba, and called there on the name of the Lord, the everlasting God.

THE NAMES OF JEHOVAH

Jehovah-Jireh –

Genesis 22:8-14

Meaning – The **Lord will see or provide** in Genesis 22:8-14 where God told Abraham to offer his son Isaac as a burn offering. This was a place in the land of Moriah, the location of the binding of Isaac where Abraham was willing to sacrifice his son. Abraham named the place after God provided a ram to sacrifice in place of Isaac.

Jehovah-Nissi –

Exodus 17:14-16

Meaning – the Hebrews name also known as the **Lord our banner**, a name given by Moses in Exodus 17:14-16 for the altar that he built to celebrate the defeat of the Amalekites.

Jehovah-Rapha –

Exodus 15:26

Meaning – the name for **Lord my Healer** in Exodus 15:26 where God revealed himself as Jehovah the Healer or the Physician that is able to heal you physically, emotionally and spiritually.

Jehovah-Shalom –

Judges 6:23-24

Meaning – Hebrew word for **Lord our Peace**

Judges 6:23-24 where an angel of the Lord came to Gideon and said,

> *"Peace be unto thee, fear not; thou shalt not die". And Gideon built an altar there unto the Lord and called it Jehovah-Shalom which* ***according*** *to scripture is located at Ophrah of the Abiezrites. The word meaning peace, completeness, harmony, wholeness, prosperity, welfare and tranquility.*

Jehovah-Tsidqenuw –

Jeremiah 23:6

Meaning – The Lord our righteousness. Jeremiah 23:6 says "In his days Judah shall be saved, and Israel shall dwell safely; and this is his name whereby he shall be called **THE LORD OUR RIGHTEOUSNESS**, which is the title given to the Messiah.

Jehovah-Mekaddishkem –

Leviticus 20:7-8

Meaning – the English translation of the Hebrew word for "I am the Lord which sanctify you, taken from Leviticus 20:7-8 as He commanded,

> *"Sanctify yourselves therefore, and be ye holy: for I am the LORD your God. And ye shall keep my statutes, and do them:* **I am the LORD which sanctify you.**

Jehovah-Sabaoth –

Luke 2:13

Meaning the **Lord of hosts**, Hebrew word meaning heavenly host in Luke 2:13;

> *And suddenly there was with the angel a multitude of the heavenly host praising God and saying, Glory to God in the highest, and on earth peace, good will toward men.*

Jehovah-Shammah –

Ezekiel 48:35

Meaning – The Lord is present (or there) as in Ezekiel 48:35;

> *"It was round about eighteen thousand measures; and the name of the city from that day shall be* **The LORD is there**.

A reference to Jerusalem, it is one of fourteen (14) names for Jerusalem.

Jehovah-Elyown –

Psalms 7:17

Meaning – the One who reigns over all the earth as the Most High God. As in Psalms 7:17;

> *I will praise the LORD according to his righteousness: and will sing praise to the name of the* **LORD most high**.

Jehovah-Rohi –

Psalms 23:1

Meaning – the Hebrew word for shepherd as in Psalms 23:1;

> **The LORD is my shepherd:** *I shall not want.*

Both the Old and New Testaments teach that lawful wants and needs will be supplied.

Jehovah-Hoseenu –

Psalms 95:6

Meaning – the source of life, creator of Adam and Eve, the one who brought thee out of bondage, as in Psalms 9:6;

O come, let us worship and bow down; let us kneel before the **LORD our maker**.

Elohim shows us how God creates out of nothing, Hoseenu shows us how God moulds it and shapes it (Adam and Eve).

Jehovah-Eloheka –

Exodus 20:2

Meaning – The one that has brought thee out of the house of bondage, as in Exodus 20:2;

I am the **LORD thy God**, *which have brought thee out of the land of Egypt.*

Jehovah-Elohay – the **Lord my God** as in Psalms 91:1-2;

Psalms 91:1-2

He that dwelleth in the secret place of the most High shall abide under the shadow of the Almighty. I will say of the LORD, He is my refuge and my fortress: my God: in him will I trust."

Psalms 91, I believe is one of the most effective scriptures in which to identify. Every verse seems to present a place where I can insert my name and see a personal need to call upon the **Lord My God**. This should be a fairly easy scripture to read, digest, meditate on, and make it a personal dedication. It is one where you can focus, read over and over until there is revelation into just how great God is and can be.

GOD THE SON – JESUS CHRIST

The Second Person of the Trinity

Emmanuel

Isaiah 9:6, Matthew 1:23

Meaning – The Christ who came to earth was God Himself.

> **Matthew 1:23** *Behold, a virgin shall be with child, and shall bring forth a son, and they shall call his name Emmanuel, which being interpreted is, God with us.*

I Am

Exodus 3:14, John 8:58

Meaning – One of the eternal names of God, and proof that He existed before Abraham.

> **John 8:58** *Jesus said unto them, Verily, verily, I say unto you, Before Abraham was, I am.*

Lord of All

Meaning – Jesus is ruler over all things and all nations. The word which God sent unto the children of Israel, preaching peace by Jesus Christ he is Lord of all.

True God

1 John 5:20

Meaning – Jesus establishes being Divine as such, His being part of the Trinity. And we know that the Son of God is come, and hath given us an understanding, that we may know him that is true, and we are in him that is true, even in his Sn Jesus Christ, This is the true God, and eternal life.

Alpha and Omega

Revelation 1:8, 22:13

Meaning – Jesus proclaims Himself to be the beginning and end of all thing.

> *I am Alpha and Omega, the beginning and the ending, saith the Lord, which is, and which was, and which is to come, the Almighty.*

GOD THE HOLY SPIRIT

Breath of The Almighty

Job 33:4

Meaning – The Holy Spirit is the life-giving breath of God

Counselor and Comforter

John 14:16, 26; 15:26 and Romans 8:26

Meaning – The Holy Spirit is our comforter; our counselor and He gives us strength when we are weak

Spirit of Counsel

Isaiah 11:2

Meaning – The Holy Spirit will give us counsel, advice and teach us as we mature in the Word

Eternal Spirit

Hebrews 9:14

Meaning – The Holy Spirit is the same the Eternal God

Free Spirit

Psalms 51:12

Meaning – The Holy Spirit is a generous and willing spirit

God

Acts 5:3-4

Meaning – The Holy Spirit is God as the Third Person of the Trinity

Good Spirit

Nehemiah 9:20

Meaning – The Spirit of God will teach us and show us how to express goodness which is one of the Fruit of the Spirit

Holy Spirit

Psalms 51:11; Luke 11:13

Meaning – God is the Spirit, He is Holy, and He is the Spirit of Holiness

Lord

1 Corinthians 3:16-17

Meaning – As the Third Person in the Trinity, the Holy Spirit is also recognized and worshipped as the Lord Thy God.

Power of the Highest

Luke 1:35

Meaning – The Spirit of God's Power, He is greatest power.

Spirit of Wisdom and Understanding; The Spirit of Counsel and Might, The Spirit of Knowledge and of the Fear of the Lord.

Isaiah 11:2, 61:1

Meaning – He is the Spirit anointed by God to preach good tidings unto the meek, he was sent to bind up the brokenhearted, to set the captives free, open the doors to them that are bound.

Spirit of Adoption

Romans 8:15

Meaning – By this Spirit of God we are made heirs of God

Spirit of Burning

Isaiah 4:4

Meaning – He is the fire of purification

Spirit of Judgment

Isaiah 4:4, 28:6

Meaning – The Spirit brings conviction and judgment.

Spirit of Christ (Jesus Christ)

Romans 8:9, 1 Peter 1:11

Meaning – The Holy Spirit is the Spirit shared between Jesus and God

Spirit of Glory

1 Peter 4:14

Meaning – The Holy Spirit always gives Glory to God

Spirit of God

Genesis 1:2, 1 Corinthians 2:11, Job 33:4

Meaning – The Holy Spirit is the Spirit of the Trinity

Spirit of Grace

Zechariah12:10, Hebrews 10:29

Meaning – The Holy Spirit is a Spirit of Grace

Spirit of Truth

John 14:17, 15:26

Meaning – the Spirit brings truths not falsehoods

Spirit of Life

Romans 8:2

Meaning – The Holy Spirit gives life

Spirit of the Living God

2 Corinthians 3:3

Meaning – The Holy Spirit is the Spirit of the One and Only True God who is the Creator of Life.

Spirit of Prophecy

Revelations 19:10

Meaning – The Holy Spirit is the inspiration for true and accurate prophecy

Spirit of the Father

Matthew 10:20

Meaning – The Holy Spirit is shared between the Father and the Son

Spirit of Revelation

Ephesian 1:17

Meaning – God reveals His truths through the Holy Spirit

MORE SCRIPTURE REFERENCES TO THE TRINITY

God (Genesis 1.1)

Lord God (Genesis 2:4-22)

Most High God (Genesis 14:18-22)

The Almighty God (Genesis 17:1; Revelation 19:15)

The everlasting God (Genesis 21:33)

The God of Heaven (Genesis 24:3)

The God of Earth (Genesis 22:43; Revelation 11:4)

The Lord God of heaven (Genesis 24:7)

God Almighty (Genesis 28.3; 43:14; 48:3)

The mighty God (Genesis 49:24)

The God of Abraham (Exodus 3:6)

The God of Isaac (Exodus 3:6)

The God of Jacob (Exodus 3:6; 2 Samuel 23:1)

I AM (Exodus 3:13-15)

God of the Hebrews (Exodus 5:3; 7:16)

God of Israel (Exodus 24:10; 34:23)
Jealous (Exodus 34:14)
God of the spirits of all flesh (Numbers 16:22; 27:16)
The God of gods (Deuteronomy 10:17)
The eternal God (Deuteronomy 33:27)
The living God (John. 3:10)
Lord God of Israel (Joshua 22:16; 24;2)
Lord God of gods (Joshua 22:22)
Strength of Israel (1 Samuel 25:29)
The Rock (2Samuel 22:32; Psalms 18:2, 31)
God of my rock (2 Samuel 22:3)
God of the rock of my salvation (2 Samuel 22:47)
The Rock of Israel (2 Samuel 23:3)
The God of David (2 Chronicles 34:3)
The righteous God (Psalms 7:9)

MORE SCRIPTURE REFERENCES TO GOD THE SON

Jesus Christ

Seed of the woman (Genesis 3:15)

Jehovah (the Lord) Genesis 19:24, Psalms 110:1-5)

Shiloh (Genesis 49:10)

The star out of Jacob (Numbers 24;17)

Prophet (Deuteronomy. 18:15, Luke 24:19)

Rock of salvation (Deuteronomy. 32:15)

Daysman (Job 9:33)

The Anointed (Psalms 2:2)

The Son (Psalms. 2:12; Hebrews 3:36)

Sanctuary (Isaiah 8:14)

Stone of stumbling (Isaiah 8:14)

Rock of offence (Isaiah 8:14)

Wonderful (Isaiah 9:6)

Counsellor (Isaiah 9:6)

The mighty God (Isaiah 9:6)
The everlasting Father (Isaiah 9:6)
The Prince of Peace (Isaiah 9:6)
Rod out of Jesse (Isaiah 11:1)
The Branch (Isaiah 11:1, Zechariah :3:8; 6:12)
An ensign of the people (Isaiah 11:10)
My Servant (Isaiah 42:1; Matthew 12:18)
My elect (Isaiah 42:1)
Polished shaft (Isaiah 49:2)
The Redeemer (Isaiah 59:20)
The angel of His presence (Isaiah 63:9)
The Lord our righteousness (Hebrews 23:6)
Plant of renown (Ezekiel 34:29)
Messiah (Daniel 9:25; John 4:25)
The Judge of Israel (Micah 5:1)
The desire of all nations (Haggai 2:7)
The man that is My fellow (Zechariah 13:7)
Refiner and purifier (Malachi 3:3)
Sun of righteousness Malachi 4:2)
Jesus Christ (note. Matthew 1;1)
The son of Abraham (Matthew. 1:1)
The son of David (Matthew. 1:1; 9:27)
Christ (Matthew 1:17; 2:4)
Jesus (Matthew 1:21, note)
Emmanuel (God with us, Matthew. 1:23)
King of the Jews (Matthew 2:2; 21:5)
Governor (Matthew 2:6)
Nazarene (Matthew 2;23)
The Son of God (Matthew 4;3)
Master (Matthew 8:19)

The Son of man (Matthew 8:20)
Physician (Matthew 9:12)
The bridegroom (Matthew 9:15)
The friend of sinners (Matthew 11:19)
The beloved (Matthew 12:18)
The sower of seed (Matthew 13:3)
The Son of the Highest (Luke 1:32)
The horn of salvation (Luke 1:69)
The dayspring (Luke 1:78)
Christ the Lord (Luke 2:11)
Savior (Luke 2:11)
The consolation of Israel (Luke 2:25)
Salvation (Luke 2:30)
Jesus of Nazareth (Luke 4:34)
Holy One of God (Luke 4:34)
The Word (John 1:1-2)
The true Light (John 1:9)
Only begotten Son (John 1:18; 3:16)
Lamb of God (John 1;29; Rev 5:6)
The King of Israel (John 1:49)
Teacher (John 3:2)
Gift of God (John 4:10)
Savior of the world (John 4:42)
The bread of God (John 6:33)
The bread of life (John 6:35, 48-51)
Light of the world (John 8:12)
Door of the sheep (John 10:7)
The good shepherd (John 10:11)
The way, the truth, the life (John 14:6)
The vine (John 15:1-8)

Lord and God (John 20:288)
Holy One and Just (Acts 3:14)
The holy child Jesus (Acts 4:27)
A Prince and a Savior (Acts 5:31)
Lord of all (Acts 10:36)
A propitiation (Romans 3:25; 1 John 2;2)
Jesus Christ our Lord (Romans 6:23)
The Deliverer (Romans 11:26)
Christ Jesus (1 Corinthians 1:2; 1 Tim 2;5)
The power of God (1 Corinthians 1:24)
The wisdom of God (1 Corinthians 1:24)
Sanctification (1 Corinthians 1;30)
Lord of glory (1 Corinthians 2:8)
Our Passover (1 Corinthians 5:7)
Spiritual Rock (1 Corinthians 10:4)
Christ the firstfruits (1 Corinthians 15:23)
The last Adam (1 Corinthians 15:45)
The second man (Adam, 1 Corinthians 15:45-47)
Image of God (2 Corinthians 4:4)
The beloved (Ephesians 1:6)
Seed of Abraham (Galatians 3;29)
Chief Cornerstone (Ephesians 2;20)
Head of the church (Colossians 1:18)
Firstborn from the dead (Colossians 1:18)
Christ Jesus our Lord (1 Timothy 1:12)
Mediator (1 Timothy 2:4-5)
The man Christ Jesus (1 Timothy 2;5)
:4Reason for all (1 Timothy 2:6)
Ransom for all (1 Timothy 2:6)
Seed of David (2 Timothy 2:8)

Lord Jesus Christ our Savior (Tit 1;4)

Brightness of His glory (Hebrews 1;3)

Express image of His person(Hebrews 1;3)

Upholder of all things (Hebrews 1:3)

Captain of salvation (Hebrews 2;10)

Captain of salvation (Hebrews 2:10)

The Apostle and High Priest of our profession (Hebrews 3;1)

Forerunner (Hebrews 6;20_

Minister of the sanctuary (Hebrews 8;2)

Testator (Hebrews 9:16-17)

Author and finish of faith (Hebrews 12;2)

Great shepherd of the sheep (Hebrews 12:2)

Shepherd and Bishop of souls (1 Peter 2:25)

Chief Shepherd (1 Peter 5:4)

Lord and Savior Jesus Christ (2 Peter 1:11)

Day star (2 Peter 1:19)

Advocate (1 John 2:1)

Jesus Christ the righteous (1 John 2:1)

Eternal Life (1 John 5:20)

Faithful witness(Revelation 1:5)

First begotten of the dead (Revelation 1:5)

Alpha and Omega (Revelation 1:8; 21:6; 22:13)

The beginning and ending (Revelation 2:8)

The first and the last (Revelation 2:8)

Morning star (Revelation 2;28)

The Amen (Revelation 3;14)

Faithful and true witness (Revelation 3;14)

Beginning of creation-the One who began creating all things through the Father (Revelation 3:14); Eph 3:9; Col 1;15-18)

Lion of the tribe of Judah (Revelation 5:5)

The Root of David (Revelation 5:5)
The Word of God (Revelation 19:13)
King of kings, Lord of lords (Revelation 19:16)
Root and offspring of David (Revelation 22:16)
Bright and morning star (Revelation 22:16)

MORE SCRIPTURE REFERENCES TO GOD THE HOLY SPIRIT

Spirit of God (22 times Gen 1:2; 41:38; Matthew 3;16; 1 Corinthians 2:11-14)

Spirit of wisdom (Ex 28:3; Dt 34:9; Isaiah 11:2; Eph 1:17

The Spirit (113 times Num 11:17; 25; Ezekiel 1;26, 2-2, Gal 6:8; Eph 2:22)

His Spirit (Num 11:29; Ps 106:33; Isaiah 48:16; Romans 8:11; 1 Corinthians 2;19; Thy Spirit (2 King 2:9; Ps 104:30; 139:7) and My Spirit (Isaiah 42:1; Acts 2;17-18)

The Spirit of the Lord (30 times, Judge 3:10; 6:34; 11-29; 13:5; 14:6, 19; 15:14; Luke 4:18, 2 Corinthians 3:17-18

The Spirit of Elijah (2 Ki 2:15; Luke 1:17)

Thy good Spirit (Neh 9:20)

Thy free Spirit (Ps 51:12)

The Spirit of judgements (Isaiah 4:4; 28:6)

The Spirit of burning (Isaiah 4:4)

The Spirit of wisdom and understanding (Isaiah 11;2)

Spirit of counsel and might (Isaiah 11:2)
Spirit of knowledge and fear of the Lord Isaiah 11:2; sp 2 Tim 1:7)
Spirit of the holy Gods (Daniel 4;8-9; 18; 5:11)
Excellent Spirit (Daniel 5:12; 6;3)
Spirit of the Gods (Daniel 5;1)
Spirit of grace and supplications (Zechariah 12:31-32; Hebrews 10:29)
The Holy ghost (89 times, Matthew 1:18-20; 3:11; 12:31-32, 28:19; 1 John 5:7)
The Spirit of your Father (Matthew 10:20)
The power of the Highest (Luke 1:35)
The Holy Spirit (1 time, Luke 11:13)
The Comforter (John 1;16, 26; 15;26)
The Spirit of truth (John 1:17; 15:26; 16:13; 1 John 4:6, 5-6)
Spirit of holiness (Romans 1;4)
Spirit of life (Romans 8:2)
Spirit of Christ (Romans 8:9; 1 Peter 1;11)
Spirit of adoption (Romans 8:15)
Spirit of the living God (2 Corinthians 3:3)
The Spirit of His Son(Galatians 4:6)
Holy Spirit of promise (Ephesians 1:13)
Spirit of wisdom and understanding (Ephesians 1:17)
Holy Spirit of God (Ephesians 4:30)
Spirit of Jesus Christ (Philippians 1:19)
The eternal Spirit (Hebrews 9:14)
The Spirit of glory (1 Peter 4:14)
The Spirit of prophecy (Revelation 19:10)

ACKNOWLEDGMENTS

Living Praise Christian Center is a church pastored by Dr. Fred L. and Linda Hodge in the Antelope Valley area of Los Angeles County. This dynamic duo are senior pastors of what is termed "One Church" in two locations in Chatsworth and Palmdale, California. The LPCC mission is simple. "Empowering and Equipping people to fulfill their purpose in Christ by growing in Faith so they can live their lives through the Power of God. Showing and sharing his unconditional love to everyone they meet."

ABOUT THE AUTHOR

Dr. Phyllis Glass was called to Ministry early in life and is a minister at Living Praise Christian Church in Palmdale, California. She has been an ordained minister and has been conducting workshops, seminars for singles, marrieds, and general congregation for more than 25 years. Dr. Glass is a dynamic teacher who is filled with the Holy Ghost and speaks with authority under the anointing of God.

Prior to becoming an author, she has been a credentialed Business Occupations Instructor with the California Department of Corrections, where she retired after ten years; Administration and Business Manager in the Aerospace industry for 23 years. She holds a Doctor of Divinity degree and a Bachelor of Science degree in Business Administration.

Dr. Glass is the mother of five adult children, two sons, Troy and Roberto; three daughters, Rejene, Stacey, and Tonya; four grandsons, Kerry, Will, Grant, and George; five granddaughters, Nicollette, Natasha, Khayla, Sara, and Erin, and two great-grandchildren, Sienna and Jalen- Christopher.

She lives in Palmdale, California.

BIBLIOGRAPHY

The Truth About the Trinity by Charles Stanley (In Touch Ministries) February 16, 2010

The Lexicon Webster Dictionary, Volume 1, pages 343 & 451

Godwin Goziem Jireh, Bible Scholar, Updated by Ingrid Harris, PhD on Existential Phenomenology & Hermeneutics, Philosophy, Updated March 6, 2019

Dakes Annotated Reference Bible, Old and New Testaments of Authorized or King James Version Text by Finis Jennings Dake

John Brown, M. A., The Bible Hub Sermons

Don Stewart, Blue Letter Bible Ministries Free Online Reference Library

Dr. David Jeremiah, The Jeremiah Study Bible on 2 Corinthians pages 1599-1602

Lisa Jones, Explaining the Holy Trinity, Joe Paprocki, Catechists Journey, Loyola Press May 5, 2015

David Peach, What Christians Want To Know – https://www.whatchristinswanttoknow.com
Article posted on July 30, 2013

Chuck Smith, Sermon Notes for Genesis 1:26-28." Blue Letter Bible. 1 May 2005. Web. 30 Oct. 2019.
<http://www.blueletterbible,org/Comm/smith_chuck/'SermonNotes_Gen/Gen_5.cfm>

Made in the USA
Las Vegas, NV
12 August 2026

52215313R10079